Songs of a Son 2

Songs of a Son 2

Preparing for the Kingdom

ROD CONNELL

TATE PUBLISHING
AND ENTERPRISES, LLC

Songs of a Son, Volume 2
Copyright © 2016 by Rod Connell. All rights reserved.

No part of this publication may be reproduced, stored in a retrieval system or transmitted in any way by any means, electronic, mechanical, photocopy, recording or otherwise without the prior permission of the author except as provided by USA copyright law.

Scripture taken from the *New King James Version*. Copyright © 1982 by Thomas Nelson, Inc. Used by permission. All rights reserved.

This book is designed to provide accurate and authoritative information with regard to the subject matter covered. This information is given with the understanding that neither the author nor Tate Publishing, LLC is engaged in rendering legal, professional advice. Since the details of your situation are fact dependent, you should additionally seek the services of a competent professional.

The opinions expressed by the author are not necessarily those of Tate Publishing, LLC.

Published by Tate Publishing & Enterprises, LLC
127 E. Trade Center Terrace | Mustang, Oklahoma 73064 USA
1.888.361.9473 | www.tatepublishing.com

Tate Publishing is committed to excellence in the publishing industry. The company reflects the philosophy established by the founders, based on Psalm 68:11,
"The Lord gave the word and great was the company of those who published it."

Book design copyright © 2016 by Tate Publishing, LLC. All rights reserved.
Cover design by Jim Villaflores
Interior design by Mary Jean Archival

Published in the United States of America

ISBN: 978-1-68352-710-7
Religion / Christian Life / Spiritual Growth
16.07.06

Dedicated to the King of kings, the Lord Jesus Christ, and for His soon return to establish His Kingdom on the earth...maranatha!

But seek first the kingdom of God and His righteousness, and all these things shall be added to you.

—Matthew 6:33

And this gospel of the kingdom will be preached in all the world as a witness to all nations, and then the end will come.

—Matthew 24:14

Contents

Introduction 15

Never Forsaken 19
Ephesian Vision 20
Sitting with Jesus 21
For My African Brother 22
Victory Awaits 23
Winemaking 24
Orphans No More 26
Outside the Door 27
Glory Alert 29
Kingdom Position 30
Like David 31
Power of the Flesh 33
Abiding Place 35
Soldiers of the Kingdom 36
Passing Through 37
The Arrows of the Lord 38
A Daily Exercise 40
The World 42

Peace of Spirit	43
The Offering of the Soul	44
Two Turnings	45
Broken Bread	46
The Fear of the Lord	47
Betrayal	49
Exchanged Lives	50
Assembly of the Firstborn	52
Ask, Seek, Knock	53
The Hidden Ones	54
A Prayer for Wind	55
Like Jacob	57
Life before Labor	59
Zion Blessings	60
More than Revival	61
Full Inheritance	62
Kingdom Dwellers	63
Early Morning Exchange	65
Fillings	66
Temperatures of Faith	67
Spiritual Malaise	69
Lingering Flesh	71
Exploring the Kingdom	73
The Glories of Grace	75
God's Will and Faith	76
Faith Transactions	77
Desert Exercises	78
Parsing the Truth	80
The Old Man and the Flesh	82
Admonishment	84

To Desire and Wait	85
Fix My Eyes	87
The Spirit or the Fire	89
Faith Returns	90
The Holy of Holies	92
Salt and Light	93
The Gospel of the Kingdom	94
The Kingdom Now	95
Two Wills to One	96
Full Belief	98
The Faith to Wait	99
Faith, Now and Later	100
Change of Perspective	101
Residues of Flesh	103
Form and Substance	105
The Death of Revivals	106
Tempered by Wisdom	107
The Crucible of the Lord	108
Primitive Appetite	109
Beyond Rest	110
The Key to Life	112
The Deeper Journey	113
He Is…	115
Unstoppable	116
Crying for the Kingdom	118
Life for Life	120
Friends to All	122
A Way Made	124
The Restraint of God	125
Let Christ Be Christ	127

Ever-Present Help 129
Deeper Realms 131
Lingering with the Lord 133
Attitude Is Everything 135
Omniscient Creator 137
Mutual Dependence 139
The Perfection of Grace 141
Cheap Grace 142
The Trigger 143
Battle for Sovereignty 144
First Love 145
Rescue Mission 147
The Use of Will 148
Invitation 149
The Yoke of the Lord 151
Mystery Kingdom 152
Choices 154
Freed from Earth 156
Highest Praise 158
The Exchange 160
The Weapon of Surrender 162
Dealing with Flesh 164
The Path to Follow 166
Hard to Refuse 167
Deep Breathing 169
Wherever We Are 170
Call to America 171
At Ease, Soldiers! 172
Home at Last 173
The Anchor Holds 174

Builders of the Kingdom 175
Faith Is 177
A Second Chance 178
Make Him Room 179
The Top of the Morning 180
The Parables of the Fig Tree 181
Body and Head 183
Proof of Love 184
The Ingredient of Glory 185
Crying Out for More 186
Abiding in Glory 187
Hunger and Thirst 188
The Sedative of Comfort 189
Irresistible Grace* 190
Come! 192
The Purpose of Deserts 193
Full Value 194
Exploring the Kingdom 2 196
The Smallest Things 198
The Purpose of Pain 199
The Goodness of God 200
Immovable 201
The Law of the Son 202
From the Scales to Rest 203
The Danger of Distractions 205
The Mind of Christ 207
The Rewards of Patience 208
Ushers of the Kingdom 210
Springs of Glory 212
Seed Moments 214

Firsthandedness	216
Play Those Harps!	217
From Faith to Faith	219
Christ Unveiled	220
Jesus Knows	221
Looking Ahead	223
Pressing On	224
Bone and Marrow	225
Patience	226
Lest We Forget	227
His Presence	228
Artificial Fruit	229
The Poor in Spirit	231
A Return to Intimacy	232
At Hand	234
Two Songs to Sing	235
Oh, the Blood!	237
The Shade of the Cross	238
Working from Victory	239
Ever Becoming	241
What Christ Is Looking For	242
Entering In	244
Greater than Eden	246
Kingdom Renovations	248
Afterword	251

Introduction

In *Songs of a Son, Volume 1: Heart Cries along the Way*, the Holy Spirit directed me to divide the selections into four sections, the spiritual terrains all believers must pass through: mountains, valleys, wildernesses, and flatlands. Our journey is from the world to the Kingdom, with the express purpose of conforming us to the image of Christ along the way, and all the terrains are required for us to reach journey's end. Our trips to the mountains are times of revelation and inspiration, with the Holy Spirit revealing new insights and understanding of truth and the marvelous ways of the Lord. The valleys and the wildernesses are times of testing, where the enemy of our souls is allowed to try us in an effort to undo any spiritual progress we are making and for the Spirit to remove areas of flesh that are impeding that progress. The flatlands are those day-to-day times where we walk out what we have learned and made our own.

As I began to sort the poems into those categories in the first volume, I realized that the actual experiences of our walk with the Lord cannot be so neatly divided and cataloged: there is much overlap even during the course of a single day. Indeed, at times something quite unexpected happens: we might find ourselves in the mountains, riding high on fresh revelations from the Holy Spirit, when suddenly a sobering Word is given that brings us down; or we might be struggling in the wilderness, when what seems from out of nowhere, a Word of refreshing comes, lifting us (at least for the moment) out of the dry and silent place where we have been confined for days. All four of those terrains are still valid to separate for understanding's sake but how they are actually experienced is not quite so tidy. For that reason, in this volume of verse, I decided to mix them to more accurately depict our real-life travels with the Lord.

Part of the way into the book, I noticed I was giving heavy emphasis to the coming of the Kingdom, a subject that has absorbed me the past several years. The millennial reign of Christ, along with His overcomers, is the next great event on the divine timetable (temporarily delayed by the tribulation, of course)—one that has been central and precious to the heart of the Father since time immemorial. What is precious to Him should be precious to us as well. So I have added this paragraph to the original introduction and given the book the subtitle of *Preparing for the Kingdom*—again, as I sensed the prompting of the Holy Spirit. I hope you find this helpful as you read your way through the book and that the coming of the Kingdom takes on heightened significance in your heart and mind as we wait upon the return of our Savior. Our time on this earth is primarily a time of preparation for the return of the King, our return from exile in a fallen world to the fullness of the new creation.

My prayer is that you will find something herein that will help you in your own journey—words that will bring comfort, encouragement, direction, and strength in Christ to complete your course victoriously as we pass from the world to the Kingdom of our Lord.

Maranatha!

Never Forsaken

Arctic midnights and desert noons
We are called to walk alone;
Though the Spirit to ours attunes,
Only human flesh our own…

But our merciful Companion
Measures out the heat and cold,
To give us victor's dominion,
Just as holy Word foretold!

Teaching them to observe all things that I have commanded you; and lo, I am with you always, even to the end of the age. (Matt. 28:20)

No temptation has overtaken you except such as is common to man; but God is faithful, who will not allow you to be tempted beyond what you are able, but with the temptation will also make the way of escape, that you may be able to bear it. (1 Cor. 10:13)

There are certainly times when the Lord seems far away and we feel all alone to face whatever situation in which we find ourselves. If our time of trial or temptation is intense, we tend to forget the promises Christ made to us: that He would never leave nor forsake us (Heb. 13:5-6) and that He would not allow us to go through anything that would be more than we can bear. So hang on even if you don't understand why you are going through such an ordeal. Trust God. He is as close as your own heart and in due time will come with a way of escape. And when it comes, be sure to take it!

Ephesian Vision

Where Christ sits we find our true seat,
High in the heavenlies;
Place where there is never defeat,
Where we see what He sees!

This must remain our vantage point,
Satan always beneath;
This vision Spirit will anoint,
The foe under our feet!

Even when we were dead in trespasses, made us alive together with Christ (by grace you have been saved), and raised us up together, and made us to sit together in the heavenly places in Christ Jesus. (Eph. 2:5-6)

Behold, I give you the authority to trample on serpents and scorpions, and over all the power of the enemy, and nothing shall by any means hurt you. (Luke 10:19)

Victory in spiritual battles is a matter of elevation. Those in Christ have been seated in heavenly places far above all the power of the enemy. And we have been given authority over Satan and his demonic forces. Our foe ever seeks to tempt us to fight on his terms and on his turf, the earth, for he knows we are no match for him there. We must always remember our true position and only battle on resurrection and ascension ground, for there, in Christ, Satan is no match for us!

SITTING WITH JESUS

Thank You, Lord, for a front-row seat,
Right next to Yours my own;
Elevated by Your great feat,
Made worthy of a throne!

So let us now together reign
And see Your Kingdom come;
From all that is flesh I abstain,
Your perfect will be done!

> Your kingdom come, your will be done on earth as it is in heaven. (Matt. 6:10)
>
> But seek first the kingdom of God and His righteousness, and all these things shall be added to you. (Matt. 6:33)

Reread the previous poem and the scriptures and commentary that follow it; the point is well worth repeating. The coming of the Kingdom is the next great spiritual event, and the eyes of the Father have been on the Kingdom from before the foundation of the world, that He might rule the earth even as He rules heaven. For this to happen, the creation of man as God originally intended must be completed. Jesus is the first Man who has fulfilled Father's eternal purpose, and Christ is to be but the firstborn of many brothers and sisters, a new race of humanity. That is why Matthew 6:33 exhorts us to seek "first" the Kingdom and the righteousness of God that will bring it about. For those who allow Christ to be their life now, spiritually speaking, the Kingdom has already come!

For My African Brother

(For Kareem Amu)

A choice twilight guard fell today,
So intense is my grief!
But I cannot doubt, will not sway,
No erosion of belief.

He is home now, with that great cloud,
Solved, mysteries of earth...
I must fight on in time allowed,
Battle for Kingdom's birth!

> Therefore, since all these things will be dissolved, what manner of persons ought you to be in holy conduct and godliness, looking for and hastening the coming of the day of God. (1 Pet. 3:11-12a)

We must come to realize that we play a part in the coming of the Kingdom: we can either hasten or delay its coming! By submitting our will to the will of Christ in all things, we hasten its coming; this is the "battle" we must fight! By remaining independent, we delay its coming; our "holy conduct and godliness" must be Christ. My African brother in the Lord, who has gone on before us, used to say we are the "twilight guard" who must usher in the Kingdom. I miss him very much for we were definitely brothers-in-arms; but the battle continues, and we all must do our part to hasten the coming of the "day of God" and our reunion with Christ and our brothers and sisters in the Lord. See you soon, Kareem!

~ Rod Connell

Victory Awaits

More consciousness of Christ within,
This is our greatest need;
Not only to forsake all sin,
But to His Life concede.

No other way to victory,
For Kingdom to arrive…
Life swallowed the last enemy,
Eternally alive!

For without Me you can do nothing. (John 15:5b)

I have been crucified with Christ; it is no longer I who live, but Christ lives in me; and the life which I now live in the flesh I live by faith in the Son of God, who loved me and gave Himself for me. (Gal. 2:20)

Christ is to be our life—Christ Himself, not His teachings and the lessons of Scripture, which we learn and try to apply. Jesus declared that *He* is the life. He told Mary, sister of Lazarus, that *He* is the resurrection—not that one day He will resurrect the dead but that He Himself is the resurrection. Indeed He is all things spiritual; outside Him, holiness, long-suffering, patience, and all other spiritual virtues are just empty words, the labels of man, things to which men vainly aspire. But outside Christ, they simply do not exist! Christ is all in all and the sum of all things.

Oh that we might come to truly see this!

Winemaking

A church that no life contains
Like wineskin with no wine;
Wine with no skin also remains
Outside Spirit's design:

Dead is wineskin with no wine,
Wine with no wineskin loss;
First wine, then skin to confine,
Both the work of the Cross.

> Nor do they put new wine into old wineskins, or else the wineskins break, the wine is spilled, and the wineskins are ruined. But they put new wine into new wineskins, and both are preserved. (Matt. 9:17)

This passage stresses the old and the new: new wine and new wineskins, new wine and old wineskins. But equally true are wineskins with no wine or wine with no wineskins. Jesus was stressing the difference between His gospel of grace and the old Mosaic law: when the new comes, it is necessary for its "container" to also be new; the old must go. What I am stressing is a church with the Life of Christ absent or restricted and the Life of Christ finding nowhere to be deposited and work. This is the case in much of the church world today. The Holy Spirit, using the Cross, is the answer to both problems. The wine (Life of Christ) must come first, the Spirit's work in individual believers, then the wineskin, a group of such people coming together as a body, in community. Of course, churches that will not receive the Life of Christ (due to doctrine, tradition, etc.) have indeed become old wineskins as well and cannot hold new wine.

Orphans No More

We must learn to abandon
Our orphan mentality;
We're adopted daughter, son,
Father's for eternity!

Rights of one natural born,
Bestowed by elder Brother;
Cherished now, no more forlorn,
Kindred of one another!

> Just as He chose us in Him before the foundation of the world, that we should be holy and without blame before Him in love, having predestined us in adoption as sons by Jesus Christ to Himself, according to the good pleasure of His will, to the praise of the glory of His grace, by which He made us accepted in the Beloved. (Eph. 1:4-6)

Since man became estranged from his heavenly Father, he has had an orphan's mentality; a sense of not really belonging or being complete. Even with good earthly fathers, this way of thinking and feeling has persisted. For we were created in the image and likeness of God; He is our true Father. Blaise Pascal put it this way: "In the heart of every man is a God-shaped void that no created thing can fill but only God Himself." But once we understand that we are now adopted children of God, brothers and sisters of Christ Himself, this orphan mentality should fall away: we are heirs and joint-heirs with Christ! We *do* belong; we now *are* complete. Let us rise up into the full inheritance of who we are!

Outside the Door

I asked and You freely gave,
Sought and did surely find;
Now I stand here knocking, Lord,
To see what lies behind...

Is this door part of the husk
I have yet to surrender?
How long this lingering dusk,
How long till I can enter?

> To me, who am less than the least of all the saints, this grace was given, that I should preach among the Gentiles the unsearchable riches of Christ, and to make all see what is the fellowship of the mystery, which from the beginning of the ages has been hidden in God who created all things through Jesus Christ; to the intent that now the manifold wisdom of God might be made known by the church to the principalities and powers in the heavenly places, according to the eternal purpose which He accomplished in Christ Jesus our Lord. (Eph. 3:8-11)

What a passage! This is our inheritance in Christ, to know the mystery hidden in God from the beginning of the ages, that the manifold wisdom of God might confront and defeat the principalities and powers of wickedness *through the church*! Paul calls this the eternal purpose of God "which He accomplished in Christ Jesus." In Christ, this is the key and the only way for what the Father has purposed to come about...in Christ and

"Christ in us, the hope of glory," being released through us, the church…which requires the work of the Cross, removing the hard husk of self so that Christ might come through and manifest. If this does not occur, we are still living by the tree of the knowledge of good and evil, no matter how well-intentioned we are.

Glory Alert

Ever on glory alert remain:
His Presence may invade
When the last hope begins to wane,
A transfusion conveyed!

A dose of Life to carry on,
Faith's confidence renewed…
The taunts of the enemy gone,
Fresh glimpse of Kingdom viewed!

> By night on my bed I sought the one I love; I sought him, but I did not find him…I opened for my beloved, but my beloved had turned away and was gone. My heart leaped up when he spoke. I sought him, but I could not find; I called him, but he gave me no answer. (Song of Songs 3:1, 5:6)

There are times when the Lord seems to withdraw from our presence; we search and pray but are unable to find Him. These are most difficult times, but experience should teach us that He will not stay away. He has always returned in the past, and He will return again. Exactly why He has chosen to withdraw, we may or may not understand. Perhaps He is weaning us from a dependence on the feelings of glory each time we have Him to ourselves "behind the lattice." Or perhaps He has called us to deeper realms of faith and we have hesitated to respond as we counted the cost. Whatever the reason, we must hang on, for in due time we will find him again to shut the mouth of the enemy and give us "fresh glimpses of the Kingdom."

Kingdom Position

Faithful now in smallest things
Increases our domain;
Overcoming realms of self brings
The coming Kingdom's gain:

Now a time of preparation,
The time to pay the cost…
Our eternal Kingdom station
Far exceeds earthly loss!

> Nevertheless, when the Son of Man comes, will He really find faith on the earth? (Luke 18:8b)

This is a very troubling question by Jesus. It comes at the end of the parable of the widow and the unjust judge; so in that context, Christ assures His disciples that when He returns, He will indeed make things right in terms of injustice, avenging His own elect who cry out to Him day and night like the widow in the parable. The question seems to be praising the faith and persistence in prayer exhibited by the widow and to be asking if He will find that kind of faith in us when He returns. Our enemy does everything in his power to postpone the coming of the Kingdom, usually at the expense of believers. How are you holding up under his attacks and deceit? Are you faithfully praying and crying out to the Lord, paying the cost to be self-involved? Remember, He promises us greater things in the Kingdom if we are faithful now despite trials and tribulations.

LIKE DAVID

Solomon was the son of peace,
A picture of our Lord;
David fought and saw all war cease,
And Israel restored…

So like David we battle on,
Driving foes from His Land;
When God sees enemies are gone,
Kingdom will come as planned!

> So King Solomon surpassed all the kings of the earth in wisdom and riches. And all the kings of the earth sought the presence of Solomon to hear his wisdom, which God had put in his heart…Solomon reigned in Jerusalem over all Israel forty years. (2 Chron. 9:22-23, 30)

Solomon's kingdom was in many ways a foreshadowing of the millennial Kingdom of Christ. His father, King David, had defeated all the main enemies of Israel, making a way for Solomon's reign, which lasted for forty years and was a period of great peace and prosperity in Israel. (Forty is the number of testing in Scripture; but of course, after forty years, Solomon's kingdom failed, for such is the fate of all the kingdoms of man.) The chapter of 2 Chronicles 9 lists all the glory of that kingdom. We are now engaged in a great battle, even as was King David, fighting all the powers of darkness and foes of the Kingdom of Christ to come. Victory is certain so long as we remain *in Christ* and *in the Spirit*;

the Kingdom has been delayed due to much of the battle being waged in the flesh and the power of man. O Lord, may we truly come to see this! The Spirit is searching for those who will live in such a way so as to hasten His coming (2 Pet. 3:12).

Power of the Flesh

Pull of the world is strong,
But flesh is stronger yet!
Its fruits to foe belong,
So deep its roots are set!

God's sentence is to die,
Raise not again its head;
To revive, it will try,
But faith must keep it dead!

For the flesh lusts against the Spirit, and the Spirit against the flesh. (Gal. 5:17a)

O wretched man that I am! Who will deliver me from this body of death?...For the law of the Spirit of life in Christ Jesus has made me free from the law of sin and death. (Rom. 7:24; 8:2)

It has been said that we are our own worst enemy, and that is true. We certainly have Satan and demonic forces with which to contend, but if there is nothing within us that can be tempted ("hooks," I call them), then there is no way for the enemy to grab hold and pull us down. Romans 6 assures us that our "old man," our old Adamic nature has been crucified with Christ, but then Romans 7 shows us that we still battle to keep the flesh down. The answer to the dilemma comes in Romans 8: when Christ indwells us, so does the law of the Spirit of life. This new law is a higher law and has overcome the lower law of sin and death. Faith in that assurance (plus the division of soul from spirit) can keep us from resisting sin in our own power, something that can never be successfully done. Thank You, Lord!

Abiding Place

The shadow of His wings?
Intimate canopy...
'Tis here my spirit sings!
Place of perfect safety,

Protection from sun and rain,
And revelation's site...
His strength throughout the day,
His comfort all the night.

> Keep me as the apple of Your eye; hide me under the shadow of Your wings, from the wicked who oppress me, from my deadly enemies who surround me. (Ps. 17:8-9)

Like David, we too have enemies, spiritually and in the world; and the only place of safety is under the shadow of His wings, the cleft of the rock. The Lord has preserved an area for His own, a place called *resurrection ground*. So long as we abide there, Satan and his hosts cannot defeat us. The main tactic of our foe, therefore, is to lure us off that ground and to tempt us to fight him in our own power, which puts us on his turf, where he rules. We must ever be on guard and not allow this to happen.

Soldiers of the Kingdom

Willingness can His will become,
If surrendered and sincere;
Such hearts He needs for the Kingdom,
They who will do what they hear:

Ever attentive to the Head,
Ever ready to obey;
Not by their own souls are these led,
For they've given those away!

> He who finds his life will lose it, and he who loses his life for My sake will find it. (Matt. 10:39)

> I am the vine, you are the branches. He who abides in Me, and I in him, bears much fruit; for without Me you can do nothing. (John 15:5)

"Not my will, Lord, but Yours be done in all things"—this must be the way we live our life. We must lose our soul-life (*psuche*) in order to gain our true life. In that sense, we must give our soul away. This happens by the work of the Cross in our life for Matthew 10:38 tells us we must take up our Cross and follow Him if we are to be His disciple. We must live as He lived: by the Life of God. In that place, there is victory! And as true soldiers of the Kingdom, that must be our stance!

Passing Through

The way home is a broken road,
Full of detours and delays…
(Past time to leave latest abode,
But part of me still stays!)

Then the Spirit insists I go,
And so I must comply…
Just temporary camps I'll know
Till Jesus splits the sky!

Beloved, I beg you as sojourners and pilgrims. (1 Pet. 2:11a)

For we have no continuing [enduring, KJV] city, but we seek the one to come. (Heb. 13:14)

Although we know that this world has been judged and is passing away, we still struggle not settling down in it. The children of Israel suffered the same malady: Egypt (a picture of the world) was a place of captivity, and yet when they faced the difficulties of making it to Canaan (the Promised Land), they murmured and complained and even desired to return to Egypt! We often experience delays and detours along the way for the same reason, but we must keep moving on, for this is not our home!

The Arrows of the Lord

The church is to be the quiver,
With sharp arrows filled;
Holy Spirit, mighty Archer,
Targets what Father willed…

But His missiles need discipline,
Stripped, straitened by the Cross;
First comes the sharpening within,
Then Lord's gain and foe's loss!

And he said, "Open the east window"; and he opened it. Then Elisha said, "Shoot"; and he shot. And he said, "The arrow of the Lord's deliverance and the arrow of deliverance from Syria." (2 Kings 13:17)

The arrows of the Lord are mentioned many times in Scripture, and they always refer to victory due to fighting the battle against the enemy the Lord's way and in His power. Most such references occur in the Old Testament, but the Lord still has His arrows and His battle plans: we are now those arrows, and the church is to be His quiver. The problem has been that too often the arrows have not been sharpened by the work of the Cross and are therefore too dull even if the Lord's strategy has been followed; defeat has been the result. And sharpened arrows shot by the power of the flesh will fail as well. As painful as some of it is, we must allow the Cross and the Holy Spirit to complete their work in us! Then victory will most certainly be the outcome for those who have fully submitted themselves to the sharpening process, working together, and who will only follow the Lord's command.

A Daily Exercise

'Tis true we've been crucified
With Christ, on the same Cross;
Yet parts of us have not died,
Never suffered soul's loss…

For this lack, only one cure,
A singular remedy:
New man must daily endure
His renewed Calvary…

I affirm, by the boasting in you which I have in Christ Jesus our Lord, I die daily. (1 Cor. 15:31)

What did Paul mean by such a statement? We know that in Galatians 2:20, Paul declared that it was no longer he who lived but that Christ lived in Him and that the life which he then lived was "by faith" in Christ. Some have said that this does not literally mean an exchanged life, but rather a life in which the will is always surrendered to the will of Christ (a very slight difference, don't you think?) At any rate, what did that "faith in Christ" include? Certainly that the old man was crucified with Christ and that the new man was to live by the law of the Spirit of life (the indwelling Life of Christ). However, there is always the danger of the new man going down the same path traveled by the old man, the way of the tree of the knowledge of good and evil, the way of independence and making his own choices. To guard against that, Paul meant a renewed death of the soul, always deferring to Christ within and never striking out on his own, something we must decide to do as well. This is a very difficult challenge, but it is the only way to victory!

The World

A camouflaged chameleon,
Changing and blending in;
The world knows just how to beckon
And hide life-ending sin:

We hardly know we have suffered,
Subtly mesmerizing;
Deadly venom so well-buffered
We barely feel the sting…

> Do not love the world or the things in the world. If anyone loves the world, the love of the Father is not in him…the world is passing away, and the lust of it. (1 John 2:15, 17a)

We know that the world has been judged and is passing away, and yet we find it difficult to avoid loving it! Not in any ultimate way (we may say we hate it), but the world has a way of drawing us in. The flesh loves the creature comforts it has to offer, so we try walk a thin line: to have the "stuff" but avoid living by the ways of the world. That is why John says to not love "the things of the world" as well as the world itself (the world system created by Satan and fallen man); those "things" have a way of beguiling us and compromising our spiritual life in the process. So hold the things of the world lightly, never coveting more and more. Avoid allowing necessary needs to expand into avarice for luxury.

Peace of Spirit

When we determinedly decrease,
Just then can He increase;
When our soulish pursuits we cease,
Our spirits grow in peace!

Less of us and Life will ensue,
Our death gives Him release;
The dead He will with Life endue,
For they the Father please…

> He must increase, but I must decrease. (John 3:30)

> The peace of God, which surpasses all understanding, will guard your hearts and minds through Christ Jesus. (Phil. 4:7)

We all desire peace—peace of mind, heart, and spirit. Much of what we strive for is indeed motivated by our need for peace. But ironically, it is only when we stop striving in our own efforts that we find peace—hence "peace that passes understanding" (KJV). John the Baptist spoke well when he said he had to decrease and Christ increase: the two things are very closely related. In fact, unless this process takes place, we will find no lasting peace. As we surrender to God in all things, it greatly pleases Him, and peace within and without is the result. Peace with God brings peace to us.

The Offering of the Soul

> Breaking of the soul's slate-hard shell
> Very work of the Cross;
> But voluntarily the will
> Must consent to its loss...
>
> The Lord will not take it by force,
> He simply points and woos;
> But so constraining is love's source,
> Self we mind not to lose...

> For the love of Christ compels [constrains, KJV] us, because we judge thus: that if One died for all, then all died; and He died for all, that those who live should live no longer for themselves, but for Him who died for them and rose again. (1 Cor. 5:14-15)

In the beginning of our walk with the Lord, we don't realize how much the soul (part of the flesh) interferes with spiritual progress. Even after we begin to understand, it remains difficult not to fall back on soulish efforts, especially during times of testing. Gradually, however, the love of Christ conquers the soul; His love for us creates in us such a love for Him that we desire nothing more than to please Him and do His will in all things. Hallelujah!

Two Turnings

When we turn, He to us turns,
Meeting us on our way;
When the road home the soul learns,
God comes without delay!

Even as the prodigal son
Came to himself one day,
Father still halfway will run
To greet His precious stray!

No one can come to Me unless the Father who sent Me draws him; and I will raise him up at the last day. (John 6:44)

And he arose and came to his father. But when he was still a great way off, his father saw him and had compassion, and ran and fell on his neck and kissed him. (Luke 15:20)

Unless the Father had drawn us, we would never have come to Christ in the first place; we come to love Him because He first loved us. But the drawing power of God's love does not stop there.

Even when we wander away to a far country, He continues to draw. And that draw has such power that it turns us around and we come back home, even as the prodigal son did in that powerful parable. We praise You, holy Father, that You never give up on us, that in Your saving power there is also keeping power!

Broken Bread

We too are the broken bread,
Eyes opened by each break;
Brought to Life what was dead,
More of flesh does it take…

By Communion purified,
Preparing what's to come:
Supping with the Crucified,
As Bride in the Kingdom!

> For My flesh is food indeed, and My blood is drink indeed. (John 6:55)

> The sacrifices of God are a broken spirit, a broken and contrite heart—these, O God, You will not despise. (Ps. 51:17)

Of course, the main purpose of Communion is to remember the Lord, His broken Body and shed Blood that were sacrificed for us. But it is also a time for the Body of Christ to be broken, strengthened, and purified. Brokenness is essential for any believer in his preparation for the Kingdom, no longer depending on self to do the work of the Spirit. Jesus said that His Flesh is real food and His Blood real drink—real spiritual food and drink that strengthens the spirit and weakens the flesh. So let us eat of that food and partake of that drink!

The Fear of the Lord

'Tis not the fear of punishment,
That shadow long removed;
Cast out by love our Father sent,
The Cross fear's defeat proved…

No, for us, the fear to displease,
Our love for Him constrains!
Nothing done so the Spirit grieves…
This bond of love remains.

> The fear of the Lord is the beginning of knowledge, but fools despise wisdom and instruction. (Prov. 1:7)

> The fear of the Lord is the beginning of wisdom, and the knowledge of the Holy One is understanding. (Prov. 9:10)

Fear of condemnation and judgment has often turned a sinner from his ways, and nothing is wrong with that as an initial motive for turning to God. But that kind of fear is gradually transformed. Once a believer begins to experience the love of God and realizes that he is eternally secure in his salvation, that original fear becomes the fear of falling short and not pleasing God. As the love of God invades the heart in ever-increasing waves, a constraining element develops. The believer's own love for the Lord begins to destroy even the desire to sin, and a mutual bond of love grows and grows. This is what Proverbs 9:10 calls "the knowledge of the Holy One"; and with that understanding, godly wisdom is imparted, the wisdom to desire the will of the Lord in all things. This is what preparation for the Kingdom is all about!

Betrayal

Betrayal in myriad of ways,
But Father always the betrayed;
Eve was the first, in Eden's days,
And black seed of deceit stayed…

So whether it's husband or wife,
Or breach between lifelong friends,
Betrayal cuts off Father's Life
And back at His doorstep ends.

> He answered and said, "He who dipped his hand with Me in the dish will betray Me. The Son of Man indeed goes just as it is written of Him, but woe to that man by whom the Son of Man is betrayed! It would have been good for that man if he had not been born." (Matt. 26:23-24)

The betrayal of Jesus by Judas was the ultimate example of betrayal. The Scriptures are full of other acts of betrayal, a breach of trust that began in the Garden of Eden. Deceit is the wellspring of betrayal, and these two produce rebellion. Deceit of course takes us back to Satan, the father of all lies. David, after his great sin with Bathsheba and the murder of Uriah, got it just right when he said, "Against You, You only have I sinned, and done this evil in Your sight" (Ps. 51:4a). Returning to the thoughts of the last poem, "The Fear of the Lord," the constraining love of Christ is a great preventive against betrayal, for the believer begins to see that any sin is a betrayal of God, and that becomes the last thing he ever desires to do.

Exchanged Lives

A labyrinth, this exchange of lives:
I'm sure I've made the trade,
But then again, my own arrives,
Flesh openly displayed!

How to complete the transaction,
This my ardent prayer…
Must path be fraction by fraction,
To at long last get there?

> Then the Lord spoke to Moses and Aaron, "Because you did not believe Me, to hallow [sanctify KJV] Me in the eyes of the children of Israel, therefore you shall not bring this assembly into the land which I have given them." (Num. 20:12)

Moses's sin of striking the rock for water instead of speaking to it as God commanded had serious consequences for the great deliverer: he was not allowed to lead the people into the Promised Land! This came as quite a shock to me when I read it as a new believer. My thoughts went something like this: here was a man who had labored with his own stiff-necked people as well as outside enemies for forty years, and for this one offense he was not allowed to enter Canaan?! I simply did not understand and was greatly discouraged in my own walk with the Lord. If a man like Moses failed, how could I ever measure up? What was Moses's great sin?

Misrepresenting God, not sanctifying Him in the eyes of His people: it was Moses who was angry, not God on that occasion. Our own sanctification is a lifelong process, dying little by little, so that the Life of Christ gradually becomes our life, a process that will not be completed until Christ returns and we receive our glorified body. But in the meanwhile, we must be very careful not to misrepresent (not sanctify) God in any way.

Assembly of the Firstborn

The assembling of the firstborn
A privileged place to be;
The first rays to burst the morn,
And Christ, face to face, see!

More than enough for any loss,
Rich reward for trials;
Very finest fruit of the Cross?
His waiting arms and smiles!

These are the ones who follow the Lamb wherever He goes. These were redeemed from among men, being first-fruits to God and to the Lamb. (Rev. 14:4b)

Because you have kept My command to persevere, I will also keep you from the hour of trial which shall come upon the whole world, to test those who dwell on the earth. (Rev. 3:10)

Those who follow the Lamb wherever He goes are the very ones who keep the Word of the Lord to persevere, the ones Christ calls first fruits to God and Himself. For their reward, the Lord promises to keep them from the Great Tribulation. These are they who have already been tested by the fires of tribulations and who have passed the ordeal, totally true to God; there is no need for them to be further tested. Those who have not passed must go through greater heat in the Lord's refining furnace, a time upon the earth like no other. In the end, there will be three times of harvest: first fruits, the main harvest, and the harvest of the gleanings. May we be among those of that first harvest!

Ask, Seek, Knock

You say to ask, to seek, to knock,
Three steps of the soul's ascent;
A ladder built upon the Rock
For all pilgrims who repent:

Repentance and cries for mercy,
Ample grace at each rung;
But essential to keep searching,
Deaf to enemy's tongue!

> Ask, and it will be given to you; seek, and you will find; knock, and it will be opened to you. For everyone who asks receives, and he who seeks finds, and to him who knocks it will be opened. (Matt. 7:7-8)

There is an interesting repetition in these two verses, I believe, to emphasize the ongoing process involved. There is also a progression in the three verbs. It is indeed good to ask, but once what is asked for is given, actively seeking it is next. And once found, it only takes knocking to have opened whatever the Spirit wishes to impart. Each step gets us closer and closer to the life we need, whether it is a fresh revelation, the direction the Lord wants us to take, or whatever.

Throughout our walk with the Lord, this is a good pattern to follow. For no matter how mature we have become, there is always more to learn.

The Hidden Ones

The true man of God is hidden,
Even as one who's veiled;
Who knows all power is within,
Whose soul has failed and failed…

No need for self to be displayed,
One who is what you see;
Complete exchange of lives has made,
At home in His company!

> Set your mind on things above, not on things on the earth. For you died, and your life is hidden with Christ in God. (Col. 3:2)

Oswald Chambers in his book *My Utmost for His Highest* says, "The Spirit of God testifies to and confirms the simple, but almighty, security of the life that is 'hidden with Christ in God.'" Paul spoke of this in several places as well. We live at a time in which bigger (and therefore more noticeable) is deemed better—a bigger church, a bigger ministry, more books published. And yet Jesus said He was meek and lowly. He never lived and ministered more than a few miles from where He was born. He never wrote a book. His following was always small but then dwindled to almost no one by the time He was crucified. Don't get caught up in the hype. Just live a pure life before God and men and be content wherever the Lord chooses to place you.

A Prayer for Wind

O mighty breath of God, exhale!
Fill with Your Life earth's sails;
Hasten this craft to the Kingdom
By the blast of Your gales!

The wind's far too calm, far too long,
Slow tack to journey's end;
What can we do to make them strong?
Does air on us depend?

> Therefore, since all these things will be dissolved, what manner of persons ought you to be in holy conduct and godliness, looking for and hastening the coming of the day of God? (2 Peter 12:11-12a)

Longing for the Lord's return should be the desire of every believer, for nothing in this world is going to be right until He comes back. That longing should translate into doing everything we can to hasten His coming. The verses of 2 Peter 3:11-12 indicates that we do indeed have a central role to play in that marvelous event. Peter exhorts us to live holy lives, but what exactly is a holy life? I believe Jesus made that very clear in the Sermon on the Mount by describing the character of those who will rule and reign with Him in the Kingdom. But as we consider what He had to say, especially in the Beatitudes, we realize that no one but Christ Himself has such a character. Therefore, the only way to a truly holy life is by the indwelling Life of Christ to live itself out through us. And the only way for that to happen is by us submitting our life and will to Him—His will and His power—in all things. What a responsibility! Amen.

Like Jacob

> All our schemes, the Lord to supplant,
> Will always end in strife;
> Though His blessings be abundant,
> Much richer still His Life!
>
> So like Jacob we must submit,
> Just then do we prevail!
> No matter what we seem to get,
> Unbroken, we yet fail…

For the gifts and calling of God are irrevocable [without repentance, KJV]. (Rom. 11:29)

So He said to him, "What is your name?" He said, "Jacob." And He said, "Your name shall no longer be called Jacob, but Israel; for you have struggled with God and with men, and have prevailed." (Gen. 32:27-28)

We are all so much like Jacob! Like him, we too have gifts and callings upon our life; but instead of waiting on the Lord to work them out in His ways and timing, we decide to help Him bring them about. Jacob was a child of promise, and so are we. And our Father never revokes or repents of keeping His Word—this despite how we keep getting in the way! Jacob lived up to his name, which means "supplanter," working hard to obtain the blessings of God by his own power.

It took his ordeal at Peniel to break him of his mistake. The interesting thing to notice in all this is that God never took anything away from Jacob along the way; in fact, He kept on blessing Him! But it was only when the hip socket of Jacob was dislocated that God finally had the Jacob He was looking for; and it was in this "breaking" that God said that Jacob had prevailed! Getting the point?

Life before Labor

If our labor precedes His Life,
Efforts prove futile, vain;
Only another soul in strife,
More flesh its highest gain...

All true spiritual work must be
By the Lord energized:
He the source, the power, and He
The glory realized!

> Without Me you can do nothing. (John 15:5b)

> But we are all like an unclean thing, and all our righteousnesses are like filthy rags. (Isa. 64:6a)

God's eternal purpose is that His Son, the Lord Jesus Christ, be all in all and the sum of all things (Col. 3:11; Eph. 1:22-23; Eph. 1:8b-10). For that to be the case, it must be His Life that comes forth in all things spiritual. Flesh (our efforts, even the very best ones!) can only give birth to more flesh (John 3:6). It all must be Christ, from start to finish, for any work to be of spiritual value. Anything else, no matter how well-intentioned, are "filthy rags" and unacceptable to God.

Zion Blessings

The Lord blesses out of Zion,
Father's most holy hill;
Mighty bastion of the Son,
Highest peak of His will:

Surrendered are its inhabitants,
His Life become their own;
Keeping the Word of His patience,
They exalt Christ alone…

For the Lord has chosen Zion, He has desired it for His dwelling place. (Ps. 132:13)

The Lord loves the gates of Zion more than all the dwellings of Jacob. Glorious things are spoken of you, O city of God. (Ps. 87:2)

Zion has so many meanings—some literal, some symbolic, some mystical. Geographically, it is a hill on which Jerusalem is built and from which the city was defended in ancient times. On it was the Jewish temple, the center of spiritual life. Israel is the place chosen by God for His people to dwell, Jerusalem its capital, and Zion its true center—actually, the very center of the center in God's eyes. Jerusalem has been destroyed many times, but Zion is eternal and can never be destroyed. Zion is also used to refer to heaven, the future dwelling place of all true believers. As an idea, even ideal, it is a place in the Spirit where all its inhabitants are a part of the completed creation of man, those who have made Christ their all and fulfilled God's eternal purpose. Let us settle for (and settle in!) no place but Zion!

~ *Rod Connell*

More than Revival

Revival presupposes death,
But the Kingdom never dies!
So pray not for merely new breath,
But Kingdom to realize:

His Life never touched by defeat,
All death fully overcome;
Old patterns we must not repeat,
But learn to live the Kingdom!

> Your kingdom come. Your will be done on earth as it is in heaven. (Matt. 6:10)

It has been the Father's eternal purpose and desire to rule on earth as He does in heaven, and indeed He will when Christ returns and sets up His Kingdom on earth. But the Kingdom can already be a spiritual reality for those who allow Christ to totally rule their life now. In that sense, there is no need to wait. For that to be accomplished, the indwelling Life of Christ must be released, and His Life must become our life. Our will must be surrendered to His will, even as His will was submitted to the will of the Father when Jesus walked the earth as a man. So our need is for more than just another revival, for all revivals have eventually subsided and only served as a temporary resurgence of life with a need to be repeated. Let us pray and live so as to bring about the final revival, the one that will usher in the Kingdom!

Full Inheritance

Your full inheritance, please claim,
Live as paupers no more!
All included in His great Name
Is yours, no longer poor…

Abundant now, eternal then,
Do not settle for less:
Will and testament both within,
Release them and be blessed!

> The Spirit Himself bears witness with our spirit that we are children of God, and if children, then heirs—heirs of God and joint heirs with Christ. (Rom. 8:16-17a)

> For you are all sons of God through faith in Christ Jesus…And if you are Christ's, then you are Abraham's seed, and heirs according to the promise. (Gal. 3:26, 29)

We have settled for so much less than who we truly are in Christ. False teaching and the dumbing down of the gospel is to blame for the sad situation in which much of the church finds itself.

Christ Himself dwells within the spirit of every born-again believer, the One with *all* authority over *all* the power of the enemy! We must learn to live by that Life, for that is our inheritance, to be claimed and lived now as well as in eternity. O Holy Spirit, enlighten and burn that truth into our hearts and spirits!

~ Rod Connell

Kingdom Dwellers

The Lord a company seeks,
The Kingdom-qualified;
Who obey each time He speaks,
Who live and yet have died…

On the Mount they heard Him well,
They feed on Kingdom grain;
No fear of the hordes of hell,
Awaiting their time to reign…

For the earnest expectation of the creation eagerly waits for the revealing of the sons of God. (Rom. 8:19)

This is a faithful saying…If we endure, we shall also reign with Him. (2 Tim. 2:11a, 12a)

To Him who overcomes I will grant to sit with Me on My throne, as I also overcame and sat down with My father on His throne. (Rev. 3:21)

Who are these sons of God that creation itself is groaning for their appearance? Who are these overcomers? Revelation 2 and 3 spend a great deal of time answering these questions. They are not simply all those who have believed on Christ unto salvation; all seven churches were made up of such believers. No, Christ separates those who have simply believed from those who have believed *and* have "overcome." Overcome what? Though Satan and the power of sin comprise part of the answer to this question, the key is that these overcomers have overcome *self*. They have learned to surrender their will to the will of God and to live by the indwelling Life of Christ. There is no other way to overcome! And it is these who shall rule and reign with Christ in His Kingdom.

Early Morning Exchange

My morning vigils for release,
My will waiting for Yours;
Allowing Your life to increase,
An exchange that ensures

Victory the rest of the day…
When You come, all is well,
Grace and peace settle in to stay;
Joy beyond words to tell!

But to You I have cried out, O Lord, and in the morning my prayer comes before You. (Ps. 88:13)

Cause me to hear Your loving kindness in the morning, for in You do I trust; cause me to know the way in which I should walk, for I lift up my soul to You. (Ps. 143:8)

The early morning watch is such a critical time with the Lord—upon first awakening and not at the end of the day when we are tired and weary from the pressures of the day. (Certainly, praying as we doze off is a good thing as well, but our day is over by then and we may have failed to hold up or properly respond to the challenges of the day.) But loving and listening to the Lord the first thing in the morning (a term borrowed from a brother in the Lord) can prepare us for whatever the day has in store for us. It should be a time of surrender, decreasing so that He might increase, and a time to remind ourselves that only His will and His Life have (and will) overcome all the wiles of the flesh and the enemy. I pray that you do not neglect these precious times.

Fillings

Holy Spirit ready to fill
Where He finds empty space;
The place made by surrendered will,
And self has been erased...

But parts where any flesh remains,
He will not violate;
Until the Lord completely reigns,
Further filling must wait...

> I indeed baptize you with water unto repentance, but He who is coming after me is mightier than I, whose sandals I am not worthy to carry. He will baptize you with the Holy Spirit and fire. (Matt. 3:11)

> And do not be drunk with wine, in which is dissipation; but be filled with the Spirit. (Eph. 5:18)

There is much confusion surrounding the Holy Spirit's work in a believer. All believers have been baptized by the Holy Spirit at the moment of salvation. Without that, there is no new birth. Baptism by the Holy Spirit only happens once. But there is the filling of the Holy Spirit many times as we walk with the Lord. How much a vessel can hold depends on how empty it is; the emptier it is the more that can fill it. So it is with a believer in Christ: the more he has allowed the Holy Spirit and the Cross to cut away and separate soul (flesh) from spirit, the more the Holy Spirit can fill, cleanse, enlighten, and empower.

~ Rod Connell

Temperatures of Faith

> The Lord seeks fervency and zeal,
> Sickened by lukewarmness;
> Deepest realms with Him fires reveal,
> A passion He can bless…
>
> Like David bringing back the Ark,
> Himself he could not contain;
> But poor Michal preferred the dark…
> Barren the tepid remain.

> I know your works, that you are neither cold nor hot. I could wish you were cold or hot. So then, because you are lukewarm, and neither cold nor hot, I will vomit you out of my mouth. (Rev. 3:15-16)

> Now as the ark of the Lord came into the City of David, Michal, Saul's daughter, looked through a window and saw David leaping and whirling before the Lord; and she despised him in her heart…Therefore Michal the daughter of Saul had no children to the day of her death. (2 Sam. 6:16, 23)

In matters of the Spirit, the worst condition is one of lukewarmness, when we are neither hot nor cold in our levels of faith and enthusiasm for the things of God. When our "temperature" drops low enough, the Lord is able to reach us with revelation and conviction, bringing us to repentance and renewed commitment. But when only lukewarm, it is very difficult for Him to bring about any real change. We are simply too content and comfortable, growing complacent and not even realizing our true condition ("wretched"—Revelation 3:17 calls it!) This was the situation in the church of Laodicea (Rev. 3:14-22), and it perfectly describes much of the churchgoing world of today, especially in America. The very blessings of God have become curses! Michal, David's wife, was also a portrayal of the lukewarm. She despised David for his unbridled love and exuberance for God and stayed barren the rest of her life. The lukewarm can never bring about new life; they remain spiritually sterile.

Spiritual Malaise

*Stuck in a spiritual malaise
Takes a jolt from the Lord;
For a return to fruitful ways
Takes Him to be restored…*

*For even with an awareness
Of our true condition,
Unable to break free, much less
Much needed contrition…*

Why are you cast down, O my soul? And why are you disquieted within me? Hope in God; for I shall yet praise Him, the help of my countenance and my God. (Ps. 42:11)

But You, O Lord, are a shield for me, my glory and the One who lifts up my head. I cried to the Lord with my voice, and he heard me from his holy hill. (Ps. 3:3)

In a world where there is much tribulation for the one trying to live for Christ, it is quite easy to fall into a kind of spiritual malaise. Without knowing why, a feeling of general uneasiness can set in. The things of the Spirit just don't seem to arouse and motivate as they once did. In most cases, prayer time and Bible study begin to slip and become less regular, with no real appetite for spiritual pursuits. The danger in such cases is that an opening has been made for the enemy to usher in spiritual apathy or full-blown depression. Additionally, isolation from the Body or church community tends to develop when malaise sets in; instead of drawing on the resources of the Body, other members are avoided and no real communication regarding the problem takes place. Crying out to the Lord is the only remedy for such a condition, for as it says in Psalm 3:3, He will hear and lift our heads. So, my advice? Know these times will come and be prepared for them!

Lingering Flesh

The new nature is undefiled,
Beyond the reach of foes;
Man and God at last reconciled.
No sin the new man knows...

The old man crucified and gone,
The dead no more can sin;
'Tis the flesh that keeps hanging on
And transgressing again!

Knowing this, that our old man was crucified with Him, that the body of sin might be done away with, that we should no longer be slaves to sin. (Rom. 6:6)

Therefore, if anyone is in Christ, he is a new creation; old things have passed away; behold, all things have become new. (2 Corinthians 5:17)

And that you put on the new man which was created according to God, in true righteousness and holiness. (Ephesians 4:24)

And have put on the new man who is renewed in knowledge according to the image of Him who created him. (Col. 3:10)

For the flesh lusts against the Spirit, and the Spirit against the flesh; and these are contrary to another, so that you do not do the things that you wish. (Gal. 5:17)

I included five scriptural references because this seems to be a real problem for most believers. They sincerely desire to leave sin behind, and yet, if honest, continue to often fail. Paul struggled with the same difficulty (read Romans 7). If the old man was crucified and the new man is a new creation, "renewed in knowledge according to the image of Him who created him" (Col. 3:10) and "in true righteousness and holiness" (Eph. 4:24), why does sin persist? The answer is because the flesh continues even after salvation, and it continually "lusts against the Spirit" (Gal. 5:17); or as Paul says it in Romans 8:17, "But now it is no longer I who do it, but sin that dwells in me." It is the surviving flesh that presents the problem, not the old man or the new. It won't be until we receive our glorified body that this struggle will end. In the meanwhile, we must understand that the soul and spirit are not interchangeable terms; they are quite distinct parts in our makeup, with very different functions. A separation of the two must take place for spiritual growth to progress (Heb. 4:12). This will certainly be discussed at greater length in many other offerings as we move along.

Exploring the Kingdom

> So much in the Kingdom to explore,
> Largely uncharted land;
> Few pilgrims have been there before,
> Though forever planned…
>
> The Lord Jesus Christ the King there,
> His rule is absolute;
> If His glory we hope to share,
> No Word can we dispute.

From that time Jesus began to preach and say, "Repent, for the Kingdom of heaven is at hand." (Matt. 4:17)

Or do you not know that your body is the temple of the Holy Spirit who is in you, whom you have from God, and you are not your own? For you were bought at a price; therefore glorify God in your body and in your spirit, which are God's. (1 Cor. 6:19-20)

The book of Matthew is the gospel of the Kingdom—its coming, its characteristics, and the qualifications for taking part in it. Certainly, the millennial reign of Christ on earth will someday be a reality, but even now, certain aspects of the Kingdom should be manifesting. How else to explain the repeated command to repent for the Kingdom of heaven is "at hand"? The term "at hand" means already here or about to come. As I prayed and studied about this declaration by John the Baptist, Jesus, and the early apostles, the Holy Spirit impressed this truth upon me: the Kingdom is anywhere and at any time in which the King rules. So for those who have allowed Christ to fully reign in their lives, spiritually speaking, the Kingdom has already come for them!

The key term is *fully* reign—not partially but completely. Of course, this process will not reach its culmination while we are yet in the flesh, but Christ has made a way for a greater and greater manifestation of Kingdom Life here on earth as we increasingly submit to Him in all things. Hallelujah!

The Glories of Grace

> By eternity for eternity,
> The mind of Christ instructs;
> Not by degree, but immediately,
> Beyond what intellect deducts:
>
> Changed are the soul's components,
> Taking their rightful place;
> Allies, no longer opponents
> Of His glory and grace!

> But the natural man does not receive the things of the Spirit of God, for they are foolishness to him; nor can he know them, because they are spiritually discerned. But he who is spiritual judges all things, yet he himself is rightly judged by no one. For "who has known the mind of the Lord that he may instruct Him?" *But we have the mind of Christ.* (1 Cor. 2:14-16, emphasis mine)

Until a man is born again from above, he is limited to his natural faculties (mind, will, and emotions); his spirit is nonfunctional. And as it says in the quoted passage, the natural man does not receive the things of the Spirit of God nor can he *know* them. For it is the awakened spirit received at the moment of salvation that is enabled to commune with God. The soul is then to take its place as the steward of what the spirit receives from the Holy Spirit. This is the path that leads from glory to glory and the wonders of His grace for each new believer is part of the Body of Christ, and it is Christ who is the Head, therefore the mind of the Body.

God's Will and Faith

The will of God must be known
For faith to activate;
Without it, trust and hope alone…
On knowing, faith must wait.

Once known, the very bridge to grace,
And permission to cross;
His will and our faith, once in place,
Prevent promise's loss.

So then faith comes by hearing, and hearing by the word of God. (Rom. 10:17)

For by grace through faith you have been saved, and that not of yourselves; it is the gift of God, not of works, lest anyone should boast. (Eph. 2:8-9)

We indeed must know the will of God before we can believe, putting our faith in what we have heard. And His will for all men is poured out through His Word, the Holy Bible—from His will that none should perish but that all might be saved by Christ's death on the Cross to greater and greater realms of faith. The Holy Spirit has been sent to indwell us and to teach us all *truth*, and then by grace through faith make us recipients of the gifts He has for those who love Him, so that He might come and dwell among us as our God and we His people. So by knowing His Word and being guided by the Holy Spirit, we are enabled to come into our full inheritance in Christ. Hallelujah!

Faith Transactions

God awaits a faith transaction
Promises to release;
The only way for needed traction,
For flow to never cease…

Not enough are hope and trust,
Though commendable they be;
To prevent grace's loss, faith must
Hear from God and agree.

This of course is a continuation of the last entry, hearing from God and believing what He has said to us; a faith transaction must take place. That is why 2 Timothy 2:15 exhorts us to study the Word and, with the guidance of the Holy Spirit, to "rightly" divide it, for in it are the promises of God waiting to be released and blessed. Word and Spirit are both needed for correct understanding and discernment of what is said; one without the other leads to false teaching, or as 2:16 and 17 proclaim, "profane and idle babblings" increasing to "ungodliness"; and their message will spread like cancer, straying "concerning the truth." And of course, schisms and divisions result from such errors, and people remain bound in their sins and confusion, for it is only by knowing the truth that we are set free (John 8:32)!

Desert Exercises

Those times of extended dryness
Are not to be despised;
God seeking deeper realms to bless,
Faith and will exercised:

The will must not weaken or turn,
But by these times grow strong;
And on the shoulders of faith learn
All terrains to His love belong!

> Then Jesus was led up by the spirit into the wilderness to be tempted by the devil. (Matt. 4:1)

> Most assuredly, I say to you, a servant is not greater than his master; nor is he who is sent greater than he who sent him. (John 13:16)

> As it is written: "For your sake we are killed all day long; we are accounted as sheep for the slaughter." Yet in all these things we are more than conquerors through Him who loved us. (Rom. 8:36-37)

> And we know that all things work together for good to those who love God, to those who are called according to His purpose. (Rom. 8:28)

Shortly after Jesus was baptized by water and the Holy Spirit, He was led into the wilderness to be tested, led there by the Spirit Himself. So why should we expect it to be any different for us?

Of course, our trips to the desert are many, for there is much flesh to be burned out in us. And yet, many times we question God concerning such trials. Surely Joseph must have experienced this many times during his periods of testing and temptation, and yet Genesis 50:20 reveals that he came to understand and accept God's hand through them all: "But as for you, you meant evil against me; but God meant it for good, in order to bring it about as it is this day, to save many people alive." Shouldn't that be our attitude and reaction as well? As hard as it seems at times to go through the wilderness, in the end we will praise God for these experiences. By enduring them we are becoming more like the Lord, for even He learned obedience by the things that He suffered.

Parsing the Truth

Parsing of the finer points
Finer adjustments make;
A search the Spirit anoints,
His glory to partake!

Full truth is in the details,
Full impact in the small;
A lesser inspection fails
For Christ to be all in all!

Be diligent to present yourself approved to God, a worker who does not need to be ashamed, rightly dividing the word of truth. (2 Tim. 2:15)

Then Jesus said to those Jews who believed Him, "If you abide in My word, you are my disciples indeed. And you shall know the truth, and the truth shall make you free." (John 8:31-32)

For in it the righteousness of God is revealed from faith to faith; as it is written: "The just shall live by faith." (Rom. 1:17)

We know that we are saved by grace through faith—hearing the Word of salvation, repenting, and believing in it. But the Christian journey is to be one of passing from faith to faith, the ever deeper realms of faith, again by hearing and believing. That hearing can be by direct revelation of the Holy Spirit, but more often than not, it comes through the written Word being illumined for us by the selfsame Spirit. And for that, the studying of the Scriptures is essential. For me, a lifetime of study has revealed many nuggets of truth, but by far, the most spectacular is this one: the eternal purpose of God the Father is that His Son, the Lord Jesus Christ, be all in all, the sum of all things; that everything in creation, beginning with man, might be filled with nothing but the Life and glory of Christ! We must not be satisfied with just being saved, escaping judgment, and being destined for heaven someday, as fantastic as that is. Christ has made a way for us to fulfill His Father's eternal purpose and gain our full inheritance in Christ—an inheritance most of which can be claimed on this side of heaven by full surrender to the will of Christ and His Life that indwells us!

The Old Man and the Flesh

> The old man seems to resurrect,
> Raising up his ugly head;
> But the dead can nothing affect,
> 'Tis surviving flesh instead:
>
> The old nature is dead for good,
> But flesh continues to live;
> Provision to be understood?
> Daily Cross the Lord will give!

I say then: Walk in the Spirit, and you shall not fulfill the lust of the flesh. For the flesh lusts against the Spirit, and the Spirit against the flesh; and these are contrary to one another, so that you do not do the things that you wish. (Gal. 5:16-17)

I affirm, by the boasting in you which I have in Christ Jesus our Lord, *I die daily*. (1 Cor. 15:31, emphasis mine)

I realize we have touched on this subject before (and will again!) for if we do not understand the dynamics and inner play of the old man, sin, the flesh, the new man, and his way to victory, life will continue to be a struggle even after salvation, a dreary time of giving up seemingly everything and getting nothing back in return. But this is not the gospel! It is an aberration of the gospel, one fostered by incomplete surrender to Christ and attacks by the enemy of our souls. For true salvation in Christ includes not only forgiveness from the penalty of sin but victory over its power as well! "For the law of the Spirit of life in Christ Jesus has made me free from the law of sin and death"—so reads Romans 8:2. But this is only true if we "die" daily to our own will, if our selves are allowed to be put on the cross daily. Only then will we truly be able to say, "Not my will but yours be done." A surrendered will is the trigger that releases the law of the Spirit of life in Christ Jesus to operate!

Admonishment

Don't miss it for the world!
Such a foolish trade:
The pleasures of Egypt
Wither soon and fade,

But the Kingdom delights,
As they go, expand…
May you behold the sights
Our Father has planned!

> But as it is written: "Eye has not seen, nor ear heard, nor have entered into the heart of man the things which God has prepared for those who love Him." But God has revealed them to us through His Spirit. For the Spirit searches all things, yes, the deep things of God. (Gal. 2:9-10)

The world and its things certainly offer pleasure to the flesh, but the end thereof is destruction! Moses gave up the pleasures of Egypt for the call God placed upon his life, and we must do the same. Our Kingdom is not of this world but is of the world to come when our King returns! The first part of the passage from Galatians 2:9 is often quoted in isolation, not also finishing the thought (verse 10): "But God has revealed them to us through His Spirit." The Word is full of the revelations of what God "has prepared for those who love him." He has indeed made many great and precious promises to us—some conditional, others unconditional. We may not know *all* He has prepared, but we know enough to go His way and not the way of the world! I wouldn't miss it for the world. How about you?

To Desire and Wait

To desire and wait are the demands
Of the Spirit of revelation;
To create thirst, He understands,
Is a divine obligation,

But we must have the discipline
And patience to spend the hours,
Waiting for filling from within:
Wisdom, knowledge, untold powers!

For since the beginning of the world men have not heard nor perceived by the ear, nor has the eye seen any God besides You, who acts for the one who waits on Him. (Isa. 64:4)

Blessed are those who hunger and thirst for righteousness, for they shall be filled. (Matt. 5:6)

And I shall make an everlasting covenant with them, that I will not turn away from doing them good; but I shall put My fear in their hearts so that they will not depart from Me. (Jer. 32:40)

Even the desire to seek God comes from Him and not ourselves. As He begins to draw us to Christ, a desire for the Lord begins to grow and is rekindled again and again by the Holy Spirit for just a small taste; and then we want more! Often, that desire is tested by our willingness to wait, to be patient until He comes to us once again, taking us "behind the lattice" (Song of Songs) for greater intimacy and love. But even this willingness to wait is a gift from God, which He rewards over and over again in due time. The Scriptures are full of the blessings for those who wait upon the Lord for wisdom, knowledge, power, and much more!

Fix My Eyes

O Lord, I pray, please fix my eyes!
Too much flesh still gets in…
This, even though I realize
Lust of the eyes is sin.

Help me see all things as You do,
My sight for Yours to trade;
Fixing on only what is true,
Flesh's vision to fade…

Looking unto Jesus, the author and finisher of our faith, who for the joy that was set before Him, endured the cross, despising the shame, and has sat down at the right hand of the throne of God. (Heb. 12:2)

Your ears shall hear a word behind you, saying, "This is the way, walk in it," whenever you turn to the right hand or whenever you turn to the left. (Isa. 30:21)

The twentieth-century British pastor D. Martyn Lloyd-Jones said, "If we only spent more of our time in looking at Christ we should forget ourselves" (Ligonier Ministries, Burk Parsons). Mr. Parsons also said in the same teaching that this fixing of our eyes on Christ is "the first step and entire path of the Christian life." For Jesus declared, "*I am* the way and the truth and the life" (John 14:6, emphasis mine). Much too often we look away, distracted by the enemy, and begin to seek other answers, albeit scriptural ones, only to find that they fail. For it is only Christ who has the answers and indeed *is* the answer to all problems and questions. His Life released will solve every dilemma and answer every question!

The Spirit or the Fire

It is the Spirit or the fire:
Baptism into the Body
Or following my own desire,
A simple choice of You or me...

O Lord, let all my motives be
Directed by Your perfect heart;
With a single aim—Your glory,
From the Head all my actions start!

> I indeed baptize you with water unto repentance, but He who is coming after me is mightier than I, whose sandals I am not worthy to carry. He will baptize you with the Holy Spirit and fire. His winnowing fan is in His hand, and He will thoroughly clean out His threshing floor, and gather His wheat into the barn; but He will burn up the chaff with unquenchable fire. (Matt. 3:11-12)

The choice for mankind has ever been "God or me?" That was the choice given to Adam and Eve in the garden, and it is the choice given to every man since. Christ baptizes with the Holy Spirit all those who choose God but reserves the fire of judgment for all those who choose self. That basic choice is not only the basis of our salvation but also one that all believers face every single day of their Christian walk: God or me? Do my actions come from Christ, the Head of the Body, or do they come from my own mind, emotions, and will? Christ was victorious because He always chose the will of God and not His own. The way to victory for us comes in the same way, for there is no other!

Faith Returns

Father loves a bold withdrawal,
Overflowing His vault!
But our faith requests oft too small,
Meager returns our fault…

He invites us His goodness to test,
He longs to give us more!
So always cry out for His best,
Drawn from infinite store!

Try Me now in this, says the Lord of hosts, "If I will not open for you the windows of heaven and pour out for you such blessing that there will not be room enough to receive it. (Mal. 3:10b-11)

Give, and it will be given to you, good measure, pressed down, shaken together, and running over will be put into your bosom. For with the same measure that you use, it will be measured back to you. (Luke 6:38)

Both of these passages have to do with giving and receiving, and certainly, we should always be willing to give whatever is needed, whether it is time, prayers, money, or material goods. But we should never give anything with the motive of getting back or, even worse, as some kind of formula for getting wealthy. Rather, we should give from love and caring for others, even as the Lord loves and cares for us—or as the Word says in Matthew 6:3, "Do not let your left hand know what your right hand is doing." But when we pray for ourselves and others, let us be bold and ask faithfully, knowing that the Lord's resources are endless and that He wants to bless us with His best. We are often so modest in our requests (doubting that the Lord can or will give us more) that the returns are just as modest. Pray *big* and see what He will do! Come boldly to His throne in your time of need (Heb. 10:19).

The Holy of Holies

The veil of His Body was rent
So we might gain access
To the heart of the covenant,
Holy site of the blessed...

Seated at the Father's right hand,
With His own at His side;
From before the foundations planned,
Inheritance for which He died.

> Therefore, brethren, having boldness to enter the Holiest by the blood of Jesus, by a new and living way which He consecrated for us, through the veil, that is, His flesh. (Heb. 10:19-20)

This is an extremely interesting passage. It leaves us with a question: Was the veil separating the holy place from the holiest Satan, or was it Christ? Or was it neither in that it was sin itself? We know that it was sin that cast Adam and Eve from the garden and closeness to God, who cannot even look upon sin. And we know that it was Satan who by deceit instigated that sin, thereby creating a "veil" between man and God. That separation prevailed from the garden transgression to the coming and sacrifice of Christ. Only when His flesh was torn was the barrier removed; a way back to the very presence of God was made! Worship in Spirit and truth became a reality—not merely approaching God from afar through a system we might call religious (but not truly spiritual) but rather passing freely from the holy place to the holiest, to the very presence of God Himself!

Salt and Light

> Addition of salt is meant
> To preserve what is pure;
> Further corruption prevent
> Until the total cure!
>
> Light comes darkness to dispel,
> Revealing and burning;
> Deep enlightenment until
> No shadow of turning...

> You are the salt of the earth, but if the salt loses its flavor, how shall it be seasoned? It is then good for nothing but to be thrown out and trampled underfoot by men. You are the light of the world...Let your light so shine before men, that they may see your good works and glorify your Father in heaven. (Matt. 5:13, 16)

This passage declares that we are to be both the salt and the light to a dark and decaying world. As salt, we are to prevent further decay until the coming of Christ, who will bring the permanent cure. And as light, we are to live in such a way—as reflections of His light—so that sin will be revealed in both our own lives and the lives of others. In our own lives, true enlightenment from the Holy Spirit will not only reveal darkness and sin but also burn them out. In the case of others, we must let our own light shine so that others might desire to have what we have and begin to seek it, giving glory to God once they find it.

The Gospel of the Kingdom

> Gospels of John and Christ are the same:
> Repent, for the Kingdom is near;
> And the disciples, in His Name,
> Proclaimed that word for all to hear…
>
> So it is for us to declare
> That same gospel of the Kingdom;
> For once it reaches everywhere,
> Then the appointed end will come.

And this gospel of the kingdom will be preached in all the world as a witness to all the nations, and then the end will come. (Matt. 24:14)

Many do not distinguish between the Kingdom of heaven and the gospel spoken of throughout the book of Matthew. This is most unfortunate, for confusion arises because of this. Anytime the Kingdom is mentioned, so many think only in terms of the heavenly Kingdom, where all true believers in Christ will reside in the distant future. But the millennial Kingdom is the emphasis in Matthew: the thousand-year reign of Christ on earth. Physically, that Kingdom has not yet come. But spiritually, for those who allow Christ to reign in their hearts *now*, the Kingdom is already here! God's great desire is that it shall be *on earth* as it is in heaven, His reign total and absolute, beginning in the lives, hearts, and spirits of His people. Matthew 24:14 is speaking of *that* Kingdom, not the one after the Millennium, lasting for all eternity.

The Kingdom Now

> Kingdom has come when the King reigns,
> To all hearts who obey;
> His authority Spirit sustains…
> They choose the golden way:
>
> All promises open, unfold,
> New creation's domain!
> Riches immeasurable, untold…
> For loss, abundant gain!

In those days John the Baptist came preaching in the wilderness of Judea, and saying, "Repent, for the kingdom of heaven is at hand!" (Matt. 3:1-2)

From that time Jesus began to preach and to say, "Repent, for the kingdom of heaven is at hand." (Matt. 4:17)

And as you go, preach, saying, "The kingdom is at hand." (Matt. 10:7)

This, of course, is a follow-up to the last selection. I have repeated it for added emphasis. *Now* is the time of the Kingdom for all who surrender their souls (mind, will, and emotions) to Christ, to live before Him as He lived before the Father. John the Baptist came announcing it, Jesus preached it throughout His ministry, and the early apostles did the same. For those who understand and choose this path, Kingdom life will begin to manifest. Such a life will include suffering for His namesake, but it will also include glory and rest. Hallelujah!

Two Wills to One

To submit still requires the will:
Decision to defer;
Then the will of the Lord can fill,
And flesh cannot deter…

Melding of human and divine:
No weapon has our foe
To subvert such sublime design…
Joint victory to know!

For I have come down from heaven, not to do my own will, but the will of Him who sent Me. (John 6:38)

For without Me you can do nothing. (John 15:5b)

The will is so critical a faculty in man. By its misuse, Adam and Eve chose to go their own way rather than God's, setting into motion all of human history as we know it and getting separated from God. The will is the trigger of the actions we take, determining the course of our life. So long as we make our choices independently, we have essentially made ourselves god. In John 6:38, Jesus tells us He made no independent choices but instead submitted to the will of God in all things. And John 15:15b tells us that without Him we can do nothing. It then becomes clear that we must surrender our will to Him if we are to accomplish anything of worth. We can indeed do many things without Him, but none of them are of any spiritual value, for God has told us in Isaiah 64:6 that all of our attempts at righteousness are as "filthy rags." Therefore, it is essential that we walk as Jesus walked, always using the will to defer to the will of God as we have come to understand it, making the needed corrections as we grow closer and closer to the Lord.

Full Belief

> Spirit's fullness is always there,
> But it must be received;
> Christ's very Life He came to share,
> But it must be believed!
>
> Unspeakable glory and joy,
> No longer on our own;
> No need at all flesh to employ,
> The battle His alone!

So then faith comes by hearing, and hearing by the word of God. (Rom. 10:17)

Then all this assembly shall know that the Lord does not save with sword and spear; *for the battle is the Lord's.* (1 Sam. 17:47a, emphasis mine)

Most believers stop short of full belief simply because they do not continue to seek more and more deeply for the treasures of our full inheritance in Christ. So many things remain hidden and not heard; therefore, there is nothing in those areas to believe. How is it, for example, that we can do all things through Christ who strengthens us? How does that work? And the main reason that such believers are left to fight the enemy in their own power is the lack of knowledge of what weapons are at their disposal. We may say the battle is the Lord's, but how do we turn it over to Him in an everyday, practical way? That is why we must study, study, study and pray, pray, pray! Our Lord is not a hide-and-seek God. By direct revelation of the Holy Spirit and intimate knowledge of the Word, He will reveal Himself. Try it and see what happens!

The Faith to Wait

Only to us is the unknown,
(Though much the Spirit reveals);
The rest must be by faith alone,
The part our flesh conceals…

'Tis not till we are glorified
The clearing of the glass;
The splendor of truth magnified,
When that side comes to pass!

> For now we see in a mirror, dimly, but then face to face. Now I know in part, but then I shall know just as I also am known. (1 Cor. 13:12)

Only on this side of eternity does so much remain unknown or partially known. The Holy Spirit will reveal as much as we seek, find, and live; after all, He has come to guide us into all truth. But our own flesh and the powers of darkness work to keep us from full knowledge. Beyond that, we must not falter in our faith. Rather, we must have the faith to wait, knowing that in due time all mysteries will be uncovered and revealed, and we will be known as we are known? Wow!

Faith, Now and Later

Those who scoff now soon will praise,
His appearing revealed;
Once His Kingdom comes and stays,
Nothing need be concealed...

But even now, spirit's eyes
See the truth and believe;
Partial glory realize,
The rest by faith receive...

Knowing this first: that scoffers will come in the last days, walking according to their own lusts, and saying, "Where is the promise of His coming? For since the fathers fell asleep, all things continue as they were from the beginning of creation." But the day of the Lord *will come*. (2 Pet. 3:3-4, 10a, emphasis mine]

This is certainly a follow-up to the last selection. Hunger and thirst for righteousness. Study to show yourself approved, rightly dividing the word of truth. Obey what the Holy Spirit reveals.

Little by little, the spirit's eyes will be sharpened, faith will increase, and small portions of glory experienced—all just enough to produce confidence, hope, and trust in the rest the Father has promised. What a way to live!

Change of Perspective

Looking back, after all is clear,
Of wasted years will speak;
Those things deemed crucial will appear
Superficial to seek…

So let us the Kingdom pursue,
Things that will ever last;
Eternity always in view…
The choice will soon be past!

For our light affliction, which is but for a moment, is working for us a far more exceeding and eternal weight of glory, while we do not look at the things which are seen, but at the things which are not seen. For the things which are seen are temporary, but the things which are not seen are eternal. (2 Cor. 4:17-18)

Now he who received seed among the thorns is he who hears the word, and the cares of this world and the deceitfulness of riches choke the word, and he becomes unfruitful. (Matt. 13:22)

But seek first the kingdom of God and His righteousness, and all these things shall be added to you. (Matt. 6:33)

Satan makes sure that in this world we will be hounded by tribulations and a deluge of cares, all of which become weeds in the garden of our spiritual growth. But rather than be defeated, we should simply change our perspective, realizing that most of them have been sent as distractions by the enemy. Therefore, rather than seeing them as things to be avoided (for they will surely come!), we should see them as opportunities for growth, overcoming not only by the Blood of the Lamb and the word of our testimony but also *not loving our lives even unto death*! And above all, we should never lose a Kingdom perspective and frame of mind!

Residues of Flesh

Residues of flesh I detest!
Your grace must bring the cure...
Only You can dissolve the rest,
Leaving the inside pure.

O Lord, do whatever it takes,
Turn up the needed heat!
Distill until my will forsakes
Its weakness to repeat...

For what I am doing, I do not understand. For what I will to do, that I do not practice; but what I hate, that I do. (Rom. 7:15)

Watch and pray, lest you enter into temptation. The spirit indeed is willing, but the flesh is weak. (Matt. 26:41)

The flesh cannot be defeated by willpower because the will itself is part of the flesh! The Lord showed me many years ago that the flesh, as used in the Bible, is not limited to the purely physical, but is in fact *all* we are born with naturally, which includes our mind, will, and emotions. Only our spirit is not part of the flesh, and it must be awakened at our regeneration in order to function in spiritual matters. After our salvation experience, our soul (mind, will, and emotions) is to be a steward of our spirit, which receives its understanding, direction, and empowerment from the Holy Spirit. In Romans 7, Paul discovered the limitations of willpower—the things he willed to do he did not always do, and he often did those very things he willed not to do! The flesh is subject to the old law of sin and death and can never produce true spiritual results. But the newly awakened spirit operates by the law of the Spirit of life, which has overcome the old law of sin and death (Rom. 8:1-2). Again, what can I say but "Hallelujah!"

Form and Substance

False godliness does have a form...
But of substance devoid;
Temperature remains lukewarm,
Spirit cannot anoint.

So pray that He turns up the heat,
By His Spirit be filled;
Takes His power to be increased
To gain all Christ has willed...

But know this, that in the last days perilous times will come...having a form of godliness but denying its power. (2 Tim. 3:1, 5a)

Anytime the Holy Spirit departs from any spiritual endeavor, all that is left is a form of godliness, but one that is lacking any spiritual substance. "Ichabod" (1 Sam. 4:21) is the word in Scripture that describes this condition (literal meaning: "the glory has departed"). Many are the works that have been started in the Spirit, but over time, they have degenerated into the works of the flesh, causing the glory of the Lord to depart. The same holds true in the lives of some believers. They start their Christian walk in the power of the Holy Spirit, but little by little, aspects of the flesh invade, and their walk grows stagnant and stalls. Again, Paul was at that point at the end of Romans 7 when he cried out, "O wretched man that I am! Who will deliver me from this body of death?" (verse 24) But he found the answer! (Reread 8.) Guard against the intrusions of the flesh, especially in your spiritual walk, for John 3:6 informs us that flesh can only give birth to more flesh, never spirit.

The Death of Revivals

All revivals must surely fail
Till Christ Himself returns;
Through souls of men foe will prevail,
Only Christ truly discerns

God's perfect and sustaining will…
Flesh always gets in the way,
Well-intentioned desires that kill!
Till He comes, none can stay.

> And Ezra blessed the Lord, the great God. Then the people answered, "Amen, Amen!" while lifting up their hands. And they bowed their heads and worshiped the Lord with their faces to the ground…And all the people went their way to eat the fat, to send portions and rejoice greatly, because they understood the words that were declared to them. (Neh. 8:6, 12)

Just like in this quoted verse, all true revivals are met with brokenness, rejoicing, and vows to repent and serve the Lord wholeheartedly. But then as time goes on, the souls of men get involved, usually meant to help sustain the movement of God. This invariably leads to differences and division because such efforts, though well-intentioned, are works of the flesh. Once this happens, the fire of revival weakens and eventually goes out. Every true revival is beneficial; lost or forgotten truths are at times regained. But they all have proven bell-shaped, reaching an apex then receding and becoming in need of repetition. Not till Christ returns will this not be the case.

Tempered by Wisdom

Power must be tempered by wisdom,
Spirit taking precedence;
If not, exalting of self will come,
To Father a grave offense…

Exaltation to be Christ's alone,
He must be the all in all;
No authority of our own
In matters great or small…

> The fear of the Lord is the beginning of wisdom, and the knowledge of the Holy One is understanding. (Prov. 9:10)

> Wisdom calls aloud outside…whoever listens to me will dwell safely, and will be secure, without fear of evil…for the Lord gives wisdom…He stores up sound wisdom for the upright. (Prov. 1:20, 33, 2:6a, 7)

When the Spirit manifests powerfully, there is a tendency in man to exalt himself. So many great moves by God have been extinguished by this frailty. That is why such power is in great need of wisdom alongside. And fear of the Lord is where that wisdom is born, knowing that He alone has the authority over all spiritual matters. We can serve in the role of delegated authority, but we must always remember that our authority rests upon His. Without Him, we have no authority at all. And He alone must receive the glory for all results!

The Crucible of the Lord

Our time in the Lord's crucible,
Heat and crushing applied,
Needed for us to bend our will,
Ensure more flesh has died…

Only then are we pliable,
Soft in the Potter's hand;
Only then can the Spirit fill,
The vessel shaped as planned.

As many as I love, I rebuke and chasten. Therefore be zealous and repent. (Rev. 3:19)

O house of Israel, can I not do with you as this potter? Says the Lord. Look, as the clay is in the potter's hand, so are you in My hand, O house of Israel! (Jer. 18:6)

Throughout our life in the earth as believers, we are in need of much remolding by the Spirit, His goal being to conform us to the image of Christ. To accomplish His purpose requires both heat and pressure, some of which is painful and difficult to understand as being necessary. But we must not resist or complain; He knows what He is doing! He only rebukes and chastens those whom He loves. It is far more troubling that we should receive no disciplining by the Lord! It must always be remembered that even Jesus learned obedience by the things which he suffered (Heb. 5:8).

Primitive Appetite

The soul is still strewn
With scraps of distant past;
Residue of things thrown
Out, but crumbs last and last!

Craved by primitive flesh
Of far-off former life…
Adam saying yes to fresh,
Disguised morsels of strife!

> But now, it is no longer I who do it, but sin that dwells in me. For I know that in me (that is, in my flesh) nothing good dwells; for to will is present with me, but how to perform what is good I do not find. (Rom. 7:17-18)

Once Adam and Eve sinned, their souls became overdeveloped, taking over the role of leadership in their life, a position that the soul was never intended to assume. And even after conversion, the spirit to ascend to become central control, the soul (flesh) continues to respond to the temptations of the enemy in both the areas of overt sin and in trying to do the work of the Spirit. This aspect of the soul must die so that it can descend to its rightful place: the steward or servant of the Spirit via our spirit. That is why the division of soul and spirit is so critical (Heb. 4:12).

Beyond Rest

I have heard the call to go
Beyond rest, to a sphere
So high the space below
Swallows up all down here!

Earth ties gone, gravity
Also loosing its claim...
My new identity
I'll find, and His new Name!

There remains therefore a rest for the people of God. For he who has entered His rest has himself also ceased from his works as God did from His. Let us therefore be diligent to enter that rest, lest anyone fall according to the same example of disobedience. (Heb. 4:9-11)

He who overcomes, I will make him a pillar in the temple of My God, and he shall go out no more. I will write on him the name of My God and the name of the city of My God, the New Jerusalem, which comes down out of heaven from My God, and I will write on Him My new name. (Rev. 3:12)

Resting from our own work is the first step toward resting in God. Resting in God is based on having complete faith in all the Father and Son have said. When trials come, one who resting in God will not be shaken from that faith. And as that rest and reliance grow, an exchange begins to form: the will and life of the believer exchanged for the will and Life of Christ.

As that occurs, the believer's *position* of being seated in the heavenlies with Christ (Eph. 2:6) gradually becomes the *experience* of that position, manifesting in Kingdom Life coming forth while yet living on the earth. Such an overcomer is promised many wonderful blessings in the age to come as well (Rev. 2, 3).

The Key to Life

His Life…the most elusive thing
To capture and to live!
By far the greatest blessing
Lord Jesus came to give…

And yet our search can quickly end,
The key, of course, the will;
Upon His, not our own, depend,
Life of flesh brought to nil!

> The Spirit of truth, whom the world cannot receive, because it neither sees Him nor knows Him, but you know Him, for He dwells with you and *will be in you*. (John 14:17, emphasis mine)

This promise by Jesus is to be received and lived—the Spirit of Christ Himself dwelling in the spirit of the believer. But His Life is not there to simply help us; it is there to be released and to manifest. That is what the apostle Paul meant in Galatians 2:20 when he said, "I have been crucified with Christ; it is no longer I who live, but Christ in me; and the life which I now live in the flesh I live by faith in the Son of God, who loved me and gave Himself for me." Paul had come to see that this is the key to claiming our full inheritance in Christ, the very Life of Christ living *through* us, He who has already defeated sin, death, the flesh, and the devil. Oh, that the Body of Christ might be awakened to this marvelous truth: *Christ in me, the hope of glory!* (Col. 1:27).

~ Rod Connell

The Deeper Journey

So few take the deeper journey,
Most stay in camp, content;
Leave unexplored the mystery,
Full glory Father sent:

The Life of Jesus to indwell,
Grand triumph of the Son;
Curse of the Garden to dispel,
Satan at long last done!

But we all, with unveiled face, beholding as in a mirror the glory of the Lord, are being transformed into the same image from glory to glory, just as by the Spirit of the Lord. (2 Cor. 3:18)

For in it the righteousness of God is revealed from faith to faith; as it is written, "The just shall live by faith." (Rom. 1:17)

Satan has been very adept at shortchanging most believers concerning the full value of what Christ has accomplished on their behalf. Our enemy knows he has lost and will one day be confined to a bottomless pit for a thousand years and then to the lake of fire for all eternity. With that knowledge, he also knows his only remaining strategy is to delay that inevitability. To accomplish that end, he has worked through the souls of men to create some other "gospel," a gospel stopping short of all the riches Christ has bestowed upon His own. Following their salvation experience, most believers are content to be heaven-bound and unwittingly work in their own power to live the Christian life. A few desire more and seek more deeply for the treasures of our inheritance in Christ; they go from faith to faith and glory to glory by completely surrendering to the will of the Lord. It is these who are the overcomers and these who will usher in the Kingdom.

He Is...

Without the Way, no place to go,
Without the Life, no way to live;
Without the Truth, nothing to know...
But all three did Father give!

His Son all these very things,
So we can go, know and live;
Embodiment of all blessings...
And the grace to forgive!

Jesus said to him, "*I am* the way, the truth, and the life. No one comes to the Father except through Me." (John 14:6, emphasis mine)

Having made known to us the mystery of His will, according to His good pleasure which He purposed in Himself, that in the dispensation of the fullness of the times He might gather together in one all things in Christ, both which are in heaven and which are on earth—*in Him*. (Eph. 1:9-10, emphasis mine)

The Lord Jesus Christ Himself *is* all things spiritual. Outside Him, they simply do not exist except as the concepts and ideals of man. It is imperative that we grasp and live this great truth instead of laboring to be humble, forbearing, merciful, etc. If Christ is to be all in all and the sum of all things, everything in creation filled with His Life and His glory, it includes all spiritual virtues and attributes. His will and His Life, released, are all these very things, and they become ours by Him living through us. Any other gospel is some other "gospel."

Unstoppable

By unstoppable love pursued,
Without end, relentless;
Love by grace and mercy endued,
Seeking His own to bless…

'Tis no use to resist or run
If to Him you belong;
Tireless is the love of the Son,
Unstoppable, too strong!

To whom then will you liken God? Or what likeness will you compare to Him?…Have you not known? Have you not heard? Has it not been told you from the beginning? Have you not understood from the foundations of the earth? It is He who sits above the circle of the earth, and its inhabitants are like grasshoppers, who stretches out the heavens like a curtain, and spreads them out like a tent to dwell in. He brings the princes to nothing; He makes the judges of the earth useless. (Isa. 40:18, 21-23)

Indeed before the day was, I am He; and there is no one who can deliver out of My hand; I work, and who will reverse it? (Isa. 43:13)

What the Father, Son, and Holy Spirit have determined and ordained will come to pass no matter what man or the hosts of hell do to stop or subvert it. The ultimate will of God is unstoppable. This is true in the universal sense concerning creation and in personal and individual matters as well. We find it difficult to fully understand the concept of divine election, but the Word of God teaches it nonetheless.

Romans 8:29-31 says it this way: "For whom He foreknew, He also predestined to be conformed to the image of His Son, that He might be the firstborn among many brethren. Moreover whom He predestined, these He also called; whom He called, these He also justified; and whom He justified, these He also glorified. What then shall we say to these things? If God is for us, who can be against us?" And as Isaiah 43:13 says, "I work, and who will reverse it?" I repeat: *all* that God has ordained will come to pass. He is unstoppable!

CRYING FOR THE KINGDOM

> Knowing beginning and the end,
> Do You ever cry, Lord?
> Or do Your tears on us depend,
> Our hearts in one accord?
>
> Though we know the final outcome,
> Still, tears along the way;
> Slow, pain-filled trek to the Kingdom...
> Come, Lord! No more delay!

O God! You have taken account of my wanderings. Put my tears in Your bottle. Are they not in Your book?...This I know, that God is for me. (Ps. 56:8)

Hear my prayer, Lord, listen to my cry for help; do not be deaf to my weeping. (Ps. 39:12)

Jesus wept. (John 11:35)

Once we begin to understand God's eternal purpose and then look at the condition of the world around us, it is difficult *not* to weep. We know that in His humanity, Jesus wept at the tomb of Lazarus. But why? Certainly not for Lazarus alone, for He was about to resurrect him from the dead. Was it not for the human condition, still laboring under the law of sin and death? The Father never intended for human suffering and death to be part of His creation; He is the eternal God of life. Another time, Jesus was saddened as He surveyed Jerusalem and longed to gather its people to Himself. In Luke 13:34,

Christ declared, "O Jerusalem, Jerusalem, the one who kills the prophets and stones those who are sent to her. How often I wanted to gather your children together, as a hen gathers her brood under her wings, but you were not willing!" Christ came to bring Life, abundant as well as eternal. That is why our eyes and heart should be on the Kingdom when Christ returns, the next step toward death being done away with forever. And all that we do during our time on the earth should be aimed at "hastening His coming" (2 Pet. 3:12).

LIFE FOR LIFE

He gave His Life to give me mine,
How can I give Him less?
The old man's death Father's design,
So the new He could bless…

But the new man must die as well,
Must daily bear his cross;
The strategy that defeats hell,
Satan's eternal loss!

I have been crucified with Christ; it is no longer I who live, but Christ lives in me; and the life which I now live in the flesh I live by faith in the Son of God, who loved me and gave Himself for me. (Gal. 2:20)

I affirm, by the boasting in you which I have in Christ Jesus our Lord, I die daily. (1 Cor. 15:31)

For whoever desires to save his life will lose it, but whoever loses his life for My sake will find it. For what profit is it to a man if he gains the whole world, and loses his own soul? Or what will a man give in exchange for his soul.? (Matt. 16:25-26)

Our old sinful self, which Romans 6:6 calls our "old man," has been crucified with Christ, a fact that must be appropriated by faith. Our "new man" is part of the new creation in Christ Jesus. It is He who must live after salvation. But the new man must live by his new nature and not by his old one. That is why Paul said that he died daily. He is speaking of the Life of his new man, not allowing himself to live after the manner of his old man and making no independent choices but rather dying to that, always surrendering his will to the will of Christ. The word "life" in Matthew 16 is synonymous with "soul"; the original word in both instances is *psuche*, meaning soul-life. Think on these things.

Friends to All

Christ the greatest friend of sinners,
The worst He came to save;
No one is worthy who enters,
So His Lifeblood He gave...

We must be friends to all as well,
Grace and mercy extend;
To snatch all those who will from hell,
The curse of sin to end...

Then He went out again by the sea; and all the multitude came to Him, and He taught them. As He passed by, He saw Levi the son of Alphaeus sitting at the tax office. And He said to him, "Follow Me." So he arose and followed Him. Now it happened, as He was dining in Levi's house, that many tax collectors and sinners also sat together with Jesus and His disciples; for there were many, and they followed Him. And when the scribes and Pharisees saw Him eating with tax collectors and sinners, they said to His disciples, "How is it that He eats and drinks with tax collectors and sinners?" When Jesus heard it, He said to them, "Those who are well have no need of a physician, but those who are sick. I did not come to call the righteous, but sinners, to repentance." (Mark 2:13-17)

Jesus came to save the lost and heal the brokenhearted, which of course means everybody! But the Pharisees looked down on those of the lower classes, not interacting with them at all, thinking that to do so would make

~ Rod Connell

them "unclean." When they saw Jesus spending so much time with them, even taking meals together, they were perplexed, even outraged. How could a true man of God ever do such things? Jesus's answer to their criticism was perfect and to the point:

He only came to heal the sick, those who are well needing no treatment. The Pharisees had no idea as to their true condition, that they too were quite "ill" and in need of a spiritual physician. God is no respecter of persons, the Word declares (Acts 10:34), and neither should we be. We must be friends to all, knowing that Christ died for them just as He did for us.

A Way Made

A way made where there was no way,
This is what Christ has done;
A way back home, this time to stay,
Kingdom at last begun…

For a thousand years Satan bound,
Then into fire is cast;
Hallelujahs will forever sound,
All sin and sorrow past!

> Thus says the Lord, who makes a way in the sea and a path through the mighty waters…do not remember the former things, nor consider the things of old. Behold, I will do a new thing, now it shall spring forth; shall you not know it? I will make a road in the wilderness and rivers in the desert. (Isa. 43:16, 18-19)

Once Jesus was crucified, Satan surely believed he had ended God's attempt to rescue and redeem man. There seemed to be no other answer to the curse of sin, death, and judgment. The crucifixion, however, ironically became the answer! For only by God in human form living a perfect, sinless life and willingly sacrificing His own life could a way be made for redemption and a return to God's original plan of ruling and reigning over the earth as He does in heaven. The book of Revelation, especially chapter 20, details the judgment of Satan, his fallen host, and unbelievers. And then chapters 21-22 describes the glory that awaits those who have put their faith in Christ Jesus. Hallelujah! What a Savior!

~ Rod Connell

The Restraint of God

All-powerful and yet restrained,
Co-laboring with man;
Long-suffering He has remained,
Certain of ordained plan…

For He is all-knowing as well,
His willing hearts will come;
Limited lease of earth has hell,
Permanent His Kingdom!

If you abide in Me, and My words abide in you, you will ask what you desire, and it shall be done for you. By this My Father is glorified, that you bear much fruit; so you will be My disciples. As the Father loved Me, I have also loved you; abide in My love. (John 15:7-9)

I planted, Apollos watered, but God gave the increase. So then neither he who plants is anything, nor he who waters, but God who gives the increase. Now he who plants and he who waters are one, and each will receive his own reward according to his own labor…for we are God's fellow workers. (1 Cor. 3:6-8, 9a)

God decided to restrain Himself, and although He needs no help to bring about His eternal purposes, He chose instead to co-labor with man to that end! This is such an amazing fact that we should stop, realize the magnitude and wonder of it, then worship and glorify God. We have a part to play, a very big part, either hastening the coming of the Lord or slowing it down.

What a responsibility! We can only achieve success in such an awesome task by abiding in Him and by abiding in His love, a love as powerful as the love of the Father for Christ. Again, stop and think on these things then renew your love and commitment to the Lord.

Let Christ Be Christ

To methods men are addicted,
But life they often choke;
Spirit by the flesh restricted,
Killing the truth He spoke…

We must simply let Christ be Christ,
Not to ways be confined;
Allow our souls to be sacrificed
To find all He's designed…

And I, brethren, when I came to you, did not come with excellence of speech or of wisdom declaring to you the testimony of God. For I determined not to know anything among you except Jesus Christ and Him crucified. (1 Cor. 2:1-2)

You search the Scriptures, for in them you think you have eternal life; and these are they which testify of Me. (John 5:39)

Paul had it right! Christ and Him crucified is all we need to know. All that we have and are in Christ flows from that eternal fact. Though well-intentioned in most cases, it is the souls of men that have reduced the Life, power, and glory of Christ to methods and principles, especially *after* receiving salvation by grace through faith alone. Instead of allowing the indwelling Life of Christ to be released and to manifest, many seek to live the Christian life by following certain steps and ideas about growth in grace, striving through such means "to be like

Christ." But it is His Life living through us that is the way to victory, not trying by human efforts to be like Him. Rather, like the poem says, we should simply let Christ be Christ!

Ever-Present Help

> More subtle the higher we climb,
> More slippery the slope;
> The schemes of the foe designed
> To strike faith, deflate hope…
>
> But Christ provides ample supply
> To strengthen heart, steady feet;
> No matter what Satan would try,
> Jesus there our need to meet!

> God is our refuge and strength, a very present help in trouble. Therefore we will not fear, even though the earth be removed, and though the mountains be carried into the midst of the sea; though its waters roar and be troubled, though the mountains shake with its swelling. (Ps. 46:1-3)

The heart of man frets over many things! The mind becomes confused, and the emotions tumble into a turmoil of mixed feelings, especially when God allows trying situations to arise in our lives. Through these trials, God desires to strengthen our faith in His faithfulness, but the enemy seeks to undermine our faith and cause doubt and fear to surface in its place. The timing of God's intervention and explanation so often complicates the matter. He just doesn't seem to come quickly enough to rescue us or His solution does not really satisfy us; in fact, it often causes greater consternation! Lazarus's sisters, Mary and Martha, must have experienced all these things and more. They knew Jesus could heal their brother. But Jesus, instead of coming quickly to do so, waited until Lazarus had been dead for four days! But you remember what happened next.

Instead of healing Lazarus on this side of life, He raised him from the dead, declaring that *He Himself* is the resurrection and the life. So never doubt that He will arrive for you as well in His timing and with exactly the best solution! Once we fully understand, even if it is not until we are on the other side, we will all bow and say, "Lord, for me You have done all things well."

Deeper Realms

Deep realms require deep surrender,
Holding on to less and less;
Surgery of the Cross to enter,
So Life can heal and bless...

Cutting out all that's malignant,
With purity in its place;
Freed from flesh, glory abundant,
The surplus of His grace!

O God, You are my God; early will I seek You; my soul thirsts for You; my flesh longs for You in a dry and thirsty land where there is no water. So I have looked for You in the sanctuary, to see Your power and Your glory. Because Your lovingkindness is better than life, my lips shall praise You. Thus I will bless You while I live; I will lift up my hands in Your name...my soul follows close behind You; Your right hand upholds me. (Ps. 63:1-4, 8)

The sacrifices of God are a broken spirit, a broken and contrite heart—these, O God, You will not despise. (Ps. 51:17)

There is no doubt that our greatest enemy is not Satan but ourselves. The poison of independence from God, engendered by Adam and passed on to all succeeding generations, is indeed a most powerful deterrent to spiritual growth. It is the driving force of sin, and even after surrender to Christ and salvation, it continues to be active and potent in the life of a Christian. Instead of sinning in the old ways, it turns its activities to the very way in which God is pursued—what *I think* is the right way (as opposed to what you may think), etc., all of which leads to division and the weakening of the Body of Christ. Deeper surrender and consecration as well as true humility is the only answer to this dilemma, and God will allow us to go through much failure and even suffering until we finally are humbled and learn this lesson.

Lingering with the Lord

> More time lingering with the Lord,
> To wait until attuned;
> Telling Him how much He's adored
> Before the day's resumed…
>
> Times He looks forward to as well,
> His love to us impart;
> Taking moments to share mutual
> Deposits of the heart!

Wait on the Lord; be of good courage, and He shall strengthen your heart; wait, I say, on the Lord! (Ps. 27:14)

Rejoicing in hope, patient in tribulation, continuing steadfastly in prayer. (Rom. 12:12)

And we desire that each one of you show the same diligence to the full assurance of hope until the end, that you do not become sluggish, but imitate those who through faith and patience inherit the promises. (Heb. 6:11-12)

Most of us talk about prayer and waiting on the Lord much more than we actually do it! And the enemy will do everything he can to prevent these crucial times. That is why we must commit to a daily practice of meeting with the Lord, no matter what tries to intrude and derail them. Even Jesus made it a priority to go apart from the disciples and His other commitments to spend quiet times with His Father. What will fill those times is up to the Holy Spirit. They may be times of perfect stillness, listening only and waiting for the voice and leading of the Lord or times of high praise and adoration. Or perhaps they may be times to pour out our hearts concerning what is happening in our lives. They can even be times of intense questioning of the Lord in an attempt to better understand what is going on. The key is the *waiting*—letting Him know you are there to hear from Him and that you love Him.

ATTITUDE IS EVERYTHING

Attitude is everything,
The hinges on the door
Of Father's favor and blessing,
The grace He has in store...

No complaints, be content to wait
(He always keeps His Word!)
So whether it is early or late,
'Tis certain what you heard.

> Only let your conduct be worthy of the gospel of Christ, so that whether I come and see you or am absent, I may hear of your affairs, that you stand fast in one spirit, with one mind striving together for the faith of the gospel, and not in any way terrified by your adversaries. (Phil. 1:27-28a)

> Do all things without complaining or disputing, that you may become blameless and harmless, children of God. (Phil. 2:14-15a)

At times, our attitude is like the mercury in a thermometer: up when things are going well but down the minute the "temperature" drops. Early in our walk with the Lord, this is quite common. But as we mature, these fluctuations begin to diminish; we become more even-keeled regardless of external circumstances. As the Lord proves Himself faithful more and more, we are able to go from faith to greater faith ourselves. In the Song of Songs, as her love for the King grows, the Shulamite maiden has learned such deep trust in the King that it matters not to her what the spiritual "weather" might be: "Awake, O north wind, and come, O south! Blow upon my garden, that its spices may flow out. Let my beloved come to his garden and eat its pleasant fruits" (Song of Songs 4:16). Both the harsh times (north wind) and the pleasant (south wind) are for the maturing of the fruit we are producing for the Lord. And notice that *my* garden is h*is* garden. All conditions are for our good and His glory! May we all come to see this!

OMNISCIENT CREATOR

Before the foundations were laid,
Christ wrote the entire script!
He knew all the parts to be played,
Nothing on stage has slipped

Past His omniscient eye, nor
Has caught Him unaware;
He saw it all eons before…
He was already there!

In the beginning was the Word, and the Word was with God, and the Word was God. He was in the beginning with God. All things were made through Him, and without Him nothing was made that was made. In Him was life, and the life was the light of the world. (John 1:1-4)

O Lord, You have searched me and known me. You know my sitting down and my rising up; You understand my thoughts from afar off. You comprehend my path and my lying down, and are acquainted with all my ways. For there is not a word on my tongue, but behold, O Lord, You know it altogether. (Ps. 139:1-4)

Eternity stretches not only into the infinite future but also back into the infinite past! And the Triune God has been and is now in both places! Such concepts are difficult for the finite mind to comprehend, but they are eternal facts nonetheless. And the Father, Son, and Holy Spirit are all-knowing, so why do we ever doubt their dealings with us? We were chosen in Christ before the foundation of the world, and God's desire for us is His very best. All those facts should erase anxiety and fear, allowing us to rest in the grace and goodness of our God no matter what!

Mutual Dependence

> Without the Body, growth will stall,
> We need each other so!
> No separate part has it all,
> It takes the whole to know…
>
> Eye cannot hear, ear cannot see,
> Requires the foot to move…
> The Head, given sovereignty,
> Ordained power will prove!

> But one and the same Spirit works all these things, distributing to each one individually as He wills. For as the body is one and has many members, but all the members of that one body, being many, are one body, *so also is Christ*…for in fact the body is not one member but many. (1 Cor. 11-12, 14, emphasis mine)

The Father has ordained that believers are to function as a body—the Body of Christ—with Him as the Head and we the individual members. By ourselves, we are incomplete and ill-equipped to do the work of the Lord. But as a Body, with each part functioning as designed and equipped by the Holy Spirit and always yielding to the will and power of the Head, we cannot be defeated. The problem develops when any member acts independently or attempts to do the work of another member. Satan knows this and works hard to achieve this very thing. That is why the Word exhorts us to "keep the unity of the Spirit…There is one body and one Spirit" (Eph. 4:3-4).

We are not advised to *create* unity but to keep what already exists! Oh, that we might come to see the wisdom of God in His creation of the Body of Christ!

The Perfection of Grace

> Salvation established the root
> By which new Life may grow;
> And the growth of grace bears its fruit
> So that the world might know
>
> Christ has come to preserve His seed,
> Produce a brand new race;
> Creation sin can no more impede,
> Perfection of His grace!

You will know them by their fruits…even so, every good tree bears good fruit, but a bad tree bears bad fruit. (Matt. 7:16a, 17)

For whom He foreknew, He also predestined to be conformed to the image of His Son, *that He might be the firstborn among many brethren.* (Rom. 8:29, emphasis mine)

Salvation comes through grace by faith, God's undeserved gift to all who repent and believe. But regeneration is only the seed and root of what the Father desires to accomplish. Through Christ, the firstborn, being "planted" in the spirit of every believer, the Holy Spirit will bring forth an entirely new species, mankind as the Godhead originally planned and ordained, a creation after God's own heart, and brothers and sisters of Christ, filled with His nature and goodness. This will be the perfection of His grace!

Cheap Grace

All cheap grace Christ condemns outright,
Repentance He requires;
Saving grace more than lines to recite,
A true heart change transpires:

We must repent as well as believe,
Be willing to turn around;
'Tis certainly grace we receive…
But by repentance is found.

> Now after John was put in prison, Jesus came to Galilee, preaching the gospel of the kingdom of God and saying, "The time is fulfilled, and the kingdom of God is at hand. Repent, and believe in the gospel." (Mark 1:14-15)

> We then, as workers together with Him also plead with you not to receive the grace of God in vain. (2 Cor. 6:1)

A form of "easy-believism" has developed in recent years—so-called belief without the need for repentance. The late German theologian Dietrich Bonhoeffer called this "cheap grace" and denounced it as counterfeit. And certainly, the Scriptures do not support such a doctrine. Belief in the atoning death of Christ goes hand in hand with repentance, not only godly sorrow for sin but also the willingness to turn from it. Do not be deceived by such a teaching. Repent and believe. This is the clear teaching of the Bible.

The Trigger

Will is the trigger of release,
Potent power of Christ!
Once we allow self-will to cease,
Life of the Sacrificed

Is freed to fully manifest,
No hellish force withstand!
In God's plan we must learn to rest,
Relax in His mighty hand!

Therefore do not be unwise, but understand what the will of the Lord is…be filled with the Holy Spirit. (Eph. 5:17, 18b)

Father, if it is Your will, take this cup away from Me; nevertheless not My will, but Yours, be done. (Luke 22:42)

For good or ill, our will is the trigger of release of our actions. The will is the key to victory or the way to defeat. The original sin was to go our own way, for *us* to decide good and evil and to choose. When we come to Christ in full commitment, we no longer choose independently; rather, we surrender our will to the will of Christ and allow His perfect Life to come forth. This is a very difficult lesson for the soul to learn, but it is a crucial one if we are to grow spiritually.

Battle for Sovereignty

Flesh desires to remain sovereign,
Yield to no outside control;
But flesh the very source of sin,
Power of the fallen soul!

This battle continues to rage
Until we are glorified;
So unless the Spirit we engage,
Lost is much for which He died…

> I say then: Walk in the Spirit, and you shall not fulfill the lust of the flesh. For the flesh lusts against the Spirit, and the Spirit against the flesh; and these are contrary to one another, so that you do not do things that you wish. But if you are led by the Spirit, you are not under the law. (Gal. 5:16-18)

God desires to be sovereign over all things in our lives. But the flesh (ruled by mind, will, and emotions) resists God's rule and struggles against the Spirit to maintain control. This is a daily battle, not a once-and-done situation. That is why Paul declared that he died daily, meaning that his will surrendered each day to the will of Christ, his "flesh" in this way "dying." I am sure that like us, he failed at times but then repented and started the next day with the same approach. If we are to live victoriously, this daily submission is something we must not fail to do.

~ Rod Connell

First Love

> We seek God because He first sought,
> With His love began to draw;
> We respond to the work Christ wrought,
> Grace superseding law…
>
> But 'tis God who must initiate,
> Never the human heart;
> His great love we reciprocate,
> Give back what He must start…

No one can come to Me unless the Father who sent Me draws him; and I will raise him up at the last day. (John 6:44)

We love Him because He first loved us. (1 John 4:19)

Scripture makes clear that our salvation begins with God. Left on our own, we would never have come to repentance and belief in Christ. The Father draws those who are His. We then return the love that He first extended to us. He loved first, and we responded. But our own first love for Him is something precious, to be cherished and guarded. The church at Ephesus (Rev. 2:1-7) was greatly commended by the Lord. In fact, He found only a single fault in that gathering of believers: they had "left" their first love. But that one area of failure was enough for the Lord to say, "Remember therefore from where you have fallen; repent and do the first work, or else I will come to you quickly and remove your lampstand from its place—unless you repent" (verse 5).

Evidently, those first works were motivated and carried out by their first love, which had cooled and been left behind. Repentance and a return to that first love was the only remedy that would avert judgment.

Rescue Mission

On a search and rescue mission,
Christ came to save the lost;
Ransom required God's only Son,
Most exorbitant cost!

But He gladly agreed to pay,
So Satan had no choice;
Now, no need sin's captive to stay…
Let all mankind rejoice!

When Jesus heard it, He said to them, 'Those who are well have no need of a physician, but those who are sick. I did not come to call the righteous, but sinners to repentance.' (Mark 2:17)

For the law of the Spirit of life in Christ Jesus has made me free from the law of sin and death. (Rom. 8:2)

A close friend once asked me, "But why did Christ have to die? Wasn't there some other way?" The answer, of course, is that He indeed had to come as a man, live a perfect life, and then die in our place to end the law of sin and death that began in the Garden of Eden. There was no other way. And certainly, the Father and Holy Spirit as well as Christ knew that mankind would fail and that just such a transaction would be necessary. Christ agreed to it before the foundation of the world! And He has not only succeeded in securing our redemption, canceling the penalty of sin for all believers, but He has also made a way to escape the power of sin. Hallelujah!

The Use of Will

Our will must be exercised
From beginning to end:
To will of Christ sacrificed,
Never on itself depend…

His must ever be the source
Of every choice we make;
Only way to stay on course,
And path to Kingdom take.

Jesus said to them, "My food is to do the will of Him who sent Me, and to finish His work." (John 4:34)

And He who sent Me is with Me. The Father has not left Me alone, for I always do those things that please Him. (John 8:29)

For without Me you can do nothing. (John 15:5)

In so many passages of Scripture, Jesus makes clear the way in which He lived His life: in submission to the will of the Father and never according to His own independently. And He also indicates that is the way in which we are to live before Him. He even says that without Him we can do nothing of spiritual value. But submission of our will to His does not mean the death of our will; rather, our will remains very much alive but always actively choosing His will and way and not our own. In that process, His Life is released *through us*, and victory is certain!

INVITATION

O come and rest from your burdens,
Lay them down at His feet;
Full relief from heaviest sins...
Reserved for you a seat!

The weight He has already borne,
A load no man can bear;
Soon now, dawning of Kingdom's morn,
Eternity to share!

RSVP

Come to Me, all you who labor and are heavy laden, and I will give you rest. Take My yoke upon you and learn from Me, for I am gentle and lowly in heart, and you will find rest for your souls. For My yoke is easy and My burden is light. (Matt. 11:28-30)

But God, who is rich in mercy, because of His great love with which He loved us, even when we were dead in trespasses, made us alive together in Christ (by grace you have been saved), and raised us up together, and made us sit together in the heavenly places in Christ Jesus. (Eph. 2:4-6)

Those who will rule with Christ in the Kingdom are those who have ceased from their own work and have learned to rest in the finished and perfect work of Christ on the Cross. Our own work causes us to be weary and heavy laden, so the Lord offers us a solution: to take up His yoke (which is the will of God) and to live as He lived, submitted to the Father in all things. Living in this manner lightens our burdens for He has already borne the load for us. May we truly learn this great truth from Him and live accordingly.

The Yoke of the Lord

Being led, the yoke of Christ implies,
Surrendered to His hand;
A self-motivated life dies,
All independence banned...

The only way to find His rest,
Path directed aright;
By promised destination blessed,
All our burdens made light!

This is certainly a follow-up and elaboration of the last entry. But because it is a most difficult lesson to learn, it is well worth repeating. All self-motivation, self-empowerment, and independence must go! This is true in all of life but especially in spiritual endeavors. Christ must be the source, the Spirit must be the power, and God must be given all the glory for the results produced. Anything else is the work of man—which, spiritually speaking, can only produce "filthy rags."

Mystery Kingdom

The Kingdom now in mystery form,
Invisible to those outside;
For all within become the norm,
Who to self-will have died...

Those blessed the mystery to know
The blessings now receive:
Holy Spirit given to show
All who will just believe!

I became a minister according to the stewardship from God which was given to me for you, to fulfill the word of God, the mystery which has been hidden from ages and from generations, but now has been revealed to His saints. To them God willed to make known what are the riches of the glory of this mystery among the Gentiles: which is Christ in you, the hope of glory. (Col. 1:25-27)

And He said to them, "To you it has been given to know the mystery of the kingdom of God; but to those who are outside, all things come in parables, so that 'Seeing they may see and not perceive, and hearing they may hear and not understand; lest they should turn, and their sins be forgiven.'" (Mark 4:11-12)

Most believers think of the Kingdom as being synonymous with going to heaven someday in the distant future after their death. And certainly that aspect will come to pass, but for those who understand what

Christ taught in the book of Matthew, especially in the Sermon of the Mount, the Kingdom is already here, or at least in spiritual or mystery form. The Kingdom exists anywhere and at any time that Christ is allowed to reign! So when we submit to His Kingship, His Kingdom has arrived for us. The physical reign of Christ on earth for a thousand years precedes the new heaven and new earth at the conclusion of the Millennium; so the "Kingdom" refers to both manifestations—one with Christ here on earth for a thousand years, and the second, for all eternity, after the final judgment. With all evil and the agents of evil disposed of, righteousness becomes the way of life forevermore! But it is God's desire that we begin to experience the spiritual aspects of the Kingdom even now by obedience to the King!

Choices

Go our own way and harsh the yoke,
The rebel neck will bruise;
Obedience to all He spoke
And not the path we choose:

Narrow the way, perfectly straight,
Onward to home Christ leads;
Abundant the faithful's estate,
Designed to meet all needs.

Then to Adam He said, "Because you have heeded the voice of your wife, and have eaten from the tree of which I commanded you saying, 'You shall not eat of it': "Cursed is the ground for your sake; in toil you shall eat of it all the days of your life. Both thorns and thistles it shall bring forth for you, and you shall eat the herb of the field. In the sweat of your face you shall eat bread till you return to the ground, for out of it you were taken; for dust you are, and to dust you shall return." (Gen. 3:17-19)

Choices have ever been before man. In the Garden of Eden, Adam and Eve chose to go their own way and not God's. From that day until Christ, everything required arduous effort to achieve.

The ground still produced food, but it took hard work to bring it forth. Thorns, thistles, and weeds sprang up, insects attacked, and the fertility of the earth declined. Life became a struggle. And most tragic of all, man could not find his way back to true fellowship with

God. But in Christ, a way was made for the human and divine connection to be renewed. While many physical conditions will remain the same until Christ returns, our relationship with God has completely changed. The veil of separation has been torn, and we can approach and enter into closeness with our Maker. But again, there is the same crucial choice to make: to go His way or to go our own, even in the manner in which we worship and serve Him. That is our choice each and every day. From which tree do you choose to eat, fellow pilgrim?

Freed from Earth

How heaven itself rejoices
When one condemned repents;
Resounding angelic voices
At commuted sentence!

From a dark death row cell set free,
Eyes adjusting to light;
Anointed by Spirit to see…
Supernatural sight!

For all have sinned and fall short of the glory of God. (Rom. 3:23)

For the wages of sin is death, but the gift of God is eternal life in Christ Jesus our Lord. (Rom. 6:23)

Therefore if the Son makes you free, you shall be free indeed. (John 8:36)

Likewise, I say to you, there is joy in the presence of the angels over one sinner who repents. (Luke 15:10)

The earth will never pass away, but it will be redeemed and be made anew. As with man, it is also in a fallen condition, not as God intended at all. It currently serves as a place of imprisonment for sin and sinners, captives of Satan, and it is from this that believers are freed once salvation in Christ is experienced. Once Christ returns, the beginning of the transformation of the earth will begin. After the millennial reign of the Lord, it will be completely recreated according to the original plan and blueprint of God. Satan, sin, and death will be no more, and a planet beyond Eden will emerge! But even now, man's re-creation can begin, also to be completed after the Millennium. The Word declares we are a new creation in Christ and are being made into the likeness of our Lord and Savior, no longer imprisoned by Satan and sin and freed from both the penalty and the power of sin even now!

Highest Praise

Glory, power, and dominion
To our triumphant King…
Sin and death vanquished by the Son,
Anthems of praise we sing!

Eternal Life now guaranteed,
A seat in the Kingdom;
All shadows from the pit recede…
O come, Lord Jesus, come!

Praise the Lord! Praise God in His sanctuary; praise Him in His mighty firmament! Praise Him for His mighty acts; praise Him according to His excellent greatness! Praise Him with the sound of the trumpet; praise Him with the lute and the harp! Praise Him with the timbrel and the dance; praise Him with stringed instruments and flutes! Praise Him with loud cymbals; praise Him with crashing cymbals! Let everything that has breath praise the Lord. Praise the Lord! (Ps. 150)

What a way to end the Psalms! An exhortation for every living thing to praise the Lord! A psalm is a sacred song or hymn, and the original root meant "to play on the harp." Once we begin to realize God's eternal purpose, we find ourselves filled with praise. Like David, there is much to lament in the current condition of the world, but there is also much to praise, knowing what is to come. Once Christ returns and establishes His Kingdom, all sadness and pain will be washed away, with the new heaven and new earth after the Millennium finally being as God planned and ordained in the beginning. The anticipation of such a glorious future, which will last forever, is more than enough to praise Him now and to cry out, "Come, Lord Jesus, come!"

The Exchange

All I am for all You are,
This is what You call for;
The greatest exchange by far,
Your part infinitely more!

How can anyone say, "No,
I'm just fine as I am?"
'Tis beyond my mind to know…
Heaven's open door slam?

Behold what manner of love the Father has bestowed on us, that we should be called children of God! Therefore the world does not know us, because it did not know Him. Beloved, now we are children of God; and it has not yet been revealed what we shall be, but we know that when He is revealed, we shall be like Him, for we shall see Him as He is. And everyone who has this hope in Him purifies himself, just as He is pure. (1 John 2:1-3)

Knowing this, that our old man was crucified with Him. (Romans 6:6)

It is no longer I who live, but Christ lives in me. (Gal. 2:20)

Every believer in Christ is to experience two deaths: co-death with Christ when He was crucified, finishing off the "old man" and the willing sacrifice of the "new man" in exchange for the indwelling Life of Christ. Only the first, without the second, leads to a life of struggle and frustration, in which the believer strives to be like Christ, only to find out he cannot. The indwelling Life released is the only way to true victory and the full inheritance we have in Christ. Both deaths come by faith in the Word of God and can be borne out by actual experience.

The Weapon of Surrender

>Once our surrender is complete,
>The greater things will come;
>Christ released, foe cannot defeat,
>Nor hold back the Kingdom…
>
>But no other weapons deploy,
>His Life we must access:
>Father's plan, darkness to destroy,
>Light eternally bless!

Most assuredly, I say to you, he who believes in Me, the works that I do he will do also; and greater works that these he will do, because I go to my Father…If you ask anything in My name, I will do it. (John 14:12, 14)

I am the vine, you are the branches. He who abides in Me, and I in him, bears much fruit; for without Me you can do nothing. (John 15:5)

"Greater works than these"—what a promise! "Because I go to the Father"—this is the reason that such a marvelous thing becomes a reality. What happened when Jesus went to the Father? The Holy Spirit became available for all men to receive, the very Life of Christ Himself in this way indwelling all believers! And it is that Life being released from within believers that is enabled to do the works of God. Without it, we can do nothing, for it is the Life of Christ doing the works! It is not Christ coming alongside to help. It is Christ doing the work through us! We must abandon all other means and methods, confess we cannot do it, surrender our soul (mind, emotions, and will), attune our spirits to the Holy Spirit, and then proceed in the power of the Spirit (the Life of Christ) to accomplish the Father's will. This is exactly how Jesus lived and how we are to live as well. Pray and think on these things!

Dealing with Flesh

The flesh continues to intrude
Long after saving grace;
But its input we must exclude,
With Spirit it has no place…

Consign it to its daily cross,
Willing to let it die;
So much is gained by its loss,
And Christ is lifted high!

I say then: Walk in the Spirit, and you shall not fulfill the lust of the flesh. For the flesh lusts against the Spirit, and the Spirit against the flesh…so that you do not do the things that you wish. (Gal. 5:16-17)

I affirm, by the boasting in you which I have in Christ Jesus our Lord, I die daily. (1 Cor. 15:31)

Even after salvation, the flesh continues to operate, battling against the Spirit and what He strives to develop within us. The old man was crucified with Christ (Rom. 6:6), but the flesh is part of our makeup until we are glorified. We must therefore know how to combat those intrusions and defeat them. The key is taking every thought captive to Christ and to die daily. By this, Paul meant that we must continually submit our will to the will of the Lord, or as Jesus said, we must lose our life to find our life. The word for "life" in this passage is *psuche*, or soul-life. We must willingly give up that part of our fallen nature in favor of the new Life the Lord has imparted, for therein is our true soul, a willing steward of the spirit and no longer in charge of making the decisions in our life. Again, there is much here to meditate upon!

The Path to Follow

The will of His Father the yoke
Our Savior gladly wore;
Path directed by all God spoke:
Nothing less, nothing more…

O Father, help us do the same,
Follow Your chosen course;
Our will be worthy of Your Name,
Yours always be our source.

Come to Me, all you who labor and are heavy laden, and I will give you rest. Take My yoke upon you and learn from Me, for I am gentle and lowly in heart, and you will find rest for your souls. For My yoke is easy and My burden is light. (Matt. 11:28-30)

For I have come down from heaven, not to do My own will, but the will of Him who sent Me. (John 6:38)

Again, submission of our will to His is the key to victory! And it is the only way to enter God's rest. (See Hebrews 4.) The first step is ceasing from our own work and trying to do spiritual work in our own power by the will and strength of the soul. Undertaking the work of the Lord in this way leads to exhaustion; it simply can't be done, producing only "filthy rags." But the will of God (Father, Son, and Holy Spirit) eliminates the struggle. This is the "yoke" Christ is speaking of in Matthew 11, which is available to all believers! Praise You, Lord!

Hard to Refuse

Of His great love, its destiny,
The reason we are here;
More than just its object to be,
The center of its sphere!

Such love it is hard to refuse
(Isolation instead?)...
Meaninglessness decide to choose,
To such love remain dead?

> For God so loved the world that He gave His only begotten Son, that whoever believes in Him should not perish but have everlasting life. (John 3:16)

> Blessed be the God and Father of our Lord Jesus Christ, who has blessed us with every spiritual blessing in the heavenly places in Christ, *just as He chose us in Him before the foundation of the world*, that we should be holy and without blame before Him in love, having predestined us to adoption as sons by Jesus Christ to Himself, according to the good pleasure of His will. (Eph. 1:3-5, emphasis mine)

We who are believers are the destiny of the Father's love! It is simple and yet astounding! We have been that destiny since before the foundation of the world, chosen in Him and predestined to be adopted as sons by Christ. On what basis this choice was made is veiled in mystery, but it is a fact nonetheless. And yet many will choose not to be part of that number of blessed ones, even though God loved the whole world and everyone in it (John 3:16). It will take Christ's return to unravel and understand such marvelous things.

Deep Breathing

O dear Lord, teach me how to breathe
Deep Your rarefied air;
Filter the fears and doubts beneath,
Pure inhalations dare!

Leave the realm of the double mind,
Abandon all mixture;
Your sustaining Breath may I find,
Full Life in You ensure…

To me, who am less than the least of all the saints, this grace was given, that I should preach among the Gentiles the unsearchable riches of Christ…according to the eternal purpose which He accomplished in Christ Jesus our Lord. (Eph. 3:8, 11)

For let not that man suppose that he will receive anything from the Lord; he is a double-minded man, unstable in all his ways. (James 1:7-8)

Full faith is how we breathe deeply enough to receive fully from the Lord. We must not allow doubts or fears to "shorten" our breath. This is true wisdom from the Lord, and if we thus ask Him, He will grant us the answer to our petitions. Satan will always attempt to intrude and to diminish the returns on our prayers and work. When he does, resist him, look to the Lord, and breathe deeply from His promises!

Wherever We Are

During the heat of temptation,
Help me to surrender;
Refuse flesh's conversation,
Leave mine, Your will enter...

Remind me my choices You share,
For You dwell deep inside;
Right ones or wrong ones, You are there,
To me forever tied!

> For though we walk in the flesh, we do not war according to the flesh. For the weapons of our warfare are not carnal but mighty in God for pulling down strongholds, casting down arguments and every high thing that exalts itself against the knowledge of God, *bringing every thought into captivity to the obedience of Christ.* (2 Cor. 10:3-5, emphasis mine)

It is during temptation that we must remember to surrender to the will of Christ, for by so doing, those thoughts will be made captive to the Lord so that His will and Life might be released.

Eve's first mistake in the Garden was to enter into a conversation with Satan; this opened the door to succumb to his seduction. It is also important to remember that because we are in Christ and He is in us, we drag Him into whatever sin we allow ourselves to be drawn into. Instead, submit yourself to God. Resist the devil and he will flee! (James 4:7)

Call to America

Like Israel, we too will fall…
Judgment will surely come
Unless we heed the Spirit's call;
Ignore it and we are done!

No nation can our God desert,
And His blessings still presume;
Last resort His people to hurt…
But that day I see loom!

> Son of man, I have made you a watchman for the house of Israel; therefore hear a word from My mouth, and give them warning from Me: When I say to the wicked, "You shall surely die," and you give him no warning, nor speak to warn the wicked from his wicked way, to save his life, that same wicked man shall die in his iniquity, but his blood I will require at your hand. (Ezek. 3:17-18)

We have repeated the great mistake of Israel: forgetting God or giving Him only token attention once the blessings have begun to flow. No country in the history of the world has been so blessed as the United States of America, not even Israel. But slowly yet surely, God is being driven from our midst! We must repent before it is too late! For if we do not, judgment is sure to fall upon us just as it did upon ancient Israel, time and time again.

At Ease, Soldiers!

Not a matter of willpower,
But our choices be Yours;
There is no way to win with our
Strength, but Yours victory ensures!

Within the One who went before,
Darkness already defeated;
Learning to rest, battling no more…
Faith in where we are seated!

And he said, "Listen, all of you of Judah and you inhabitants of Jerusalem, and you, King Jehoshaphat! Thus says the Lord to you: 'Do not be afraid or dismayed because of this great multitude, for the battle is not yours, but God's.'" (2 Chron. 20:15)

But God, who is rich in mercy, because of His great love with which He loved us, even when we were dead in trespasses, made us alive together with Christ (by grace you have been saved), and raised us up together, and made us sit together in the heavenly places in Christ Jesus. (Eph. 2:4-6)

Satan has already been vanquished by Christ, and since we are His, he is a defeated foe for us as well. But we must rest and abide in His victory and not try to battle the enemy on our own. He will always try to lure us onto his turf, the earth and the willpower of man, a place where we are no match for him. It is our job to remain on resurrection ground and the Word of God, where he is no match for us!

~ Rod Connell

Home at Last

There is nowhere else to go…
(You have tried them all!)
He is still waiting, you know,
Though faint now His call.

Run to Him while you yet hear,
He won't turn away;
Greeting of embrace and tear,
Love imploring, "Stay!"

Jesus answered, "My kingdom is not of this world…now my My kingdom is not from here." (John 18:36)

All that the Father gives Me will come to Me, and the one who comes to Me, I will by no means cast out. (John 6:37)

Christ is calling His own and has been doing so by His Spirit since His time on earth and His ascension. For them, there is nowhere else to go that will bring peace and satisfaction. For most of us, we have tried everything that the world has to offer and found it meaningless. It seems a human frailty that must be pursued and understood before turning to Christ. If this describes you and your condition, turn to Him now. Wonderful things are waiting for you there!

The Anchor Holds

His righteousness is the anchor,
But our trust the tether;
Our safety forever secure,
So let not doubts sever

Your tight hold on the Lifeline:
He will never let go,
No matter the enemy's design...
Eternal assurance know!

This hope we have as an anchor of the soul, both sure and steadfast, and which enters the Presence behind the veil. (Heb. 6:19)

And lo, I am with you always, even to the end of the age. (Matt. 28:20b)

For He Himself has said, "I will never leave you nor forsake you." (Heb. 13:5b)

The anchor of our faith is secured behind the veil, in the Holy of Holies, held by Christ Himself. What could be more safe and reassuring than that? And Christ will never let go. The only thing that can separate us and cast us adrift is the tether of our faith, by allowing it to weaken and be torn by the enemy. He will send circumstances that instill doubt and fear. These we must resist, reminding Satan that he has been defeated and no longer has any hold on us. Come to know the promises of God and quote them to him. This must be your only response to him, and he will have to flee!

~ Rod Connell

Builders of the Kingdom

    It is so easy to just drift,
    Our anchor left behind;
    But cry out and Jesus will lift
    Us and our Lifeline find...

    He will never let us drift far,
    He knows just when to come;
    His Bride and beloved we are,
    Builders of the Kingdom!

Therefore, since we are receiving a kingdom which cannot be shaken, let us have grace, by which we may serve God acceptably with reverence and godly fear. For our God is a consuming fire. (Heb. 12:28-29)

But seek first the kingdom of God and His righteousness, and all these things shall be added to you. (Matt. 6:33)

Beloved, I beg you as sojourners and pilgrims, abstain from fleshly lusts which war against your soul. (1 Pet. 2:11a)

It is only when we drift and leave our anchor behind that fleshly lusts become a serious problem; Satan is always waiting for us there. When that happens, we must awaken and cry out to Jesus for He is ever waiting to rescue us. We must come to realize that we are strangers in the earth, pilgrims just passing through on our way to the Kingdom. We must seek that first and foremost, desiring for the return of our King and Savior, doing all we can to bring that about, and allowing Christ full reign in our own lives. Make that resolve and stick to it, and the Spirit will empower and direct us.

Faith Is...

> The substance is His righteousness,
> The Cross its evidence;
> With love and by faith He will bless
> All those His words convince...
>
> Those who see with the Spirit's eyes
> What natural cannot see;
> Those who to full belief arise,
> Faith is...eternity!

Now faith is the substance of things hoped for, the evidence of things not seen. (Heb. 11:1)

For by grace you have been saved through faith, and that not of yourselves; it is the gift of God, not of works, lest anyone should boast. (Eph. 2:8)

It is faith in His righteousness that saves us. We must never forget that. And that faith has been given to us by grace—a free, undeserved gift from the love of God and by Christ's death on the Cross. It is the Holy Spirit who makes all this clear to us so that we might repent and believe. And at that moment, our own spirit is awakened to life. We are born anew with Christ by His indwelling Spirit living within us. Oh, what a Savior and what a salvation!

A Second Chance

The tree of life offered again,
This time a gruesome cross;
Far less attractive than One then,
Yet still recovers loss...

The last Adam, with second chance,
Willing to pay the cost;
Blood for every circumstance
Glory of God was lost!

However, the spiritual is not first, but the natural, and afterward the spiritual. The first man was of the earth, made of dust; the second Man is the Lord of heaven. As was the man of dust, so also are those who are made of dust; and as is the heavenly Man, so also are those who are heavenly. And as we have borne the image of the man of dust, we shall also bear the image of the heavenly Man. (1 Cor. 15:47-49)

The tree of life, with life everlasting but refused by Adam and Eve in favor of self and the tree of death, has been replaced by the Cross of Christ. He is the last Adam as well as the tree of life and its fruit. And those who eat of this second tree receive both eternal and abundant Life. All of fallen mankind have been given a second chance because Christ came and was willing to suffer the judgment for their sins. Again, what a Savior and what a salvation!

Make Him Room

There is still no room for the Lord
In many crowded hearts;
The One by His Father adored
Finds locked doors and departs...

But listen, He will knock again,
His love will not give up!
He longs to cover all your sin,
To stay with you and sup...

So it was, that while they were there, the days were completed for her to be delivered. And she brought forth her firstborn Son, and wrapped Him in swaddling cloths, and laid Him in a manger, because there was no room for them in the inn. (Luke 2:6-7)

Behold, I stand at the door and knock. If anyone hears My voice and opens the door, I will come in to him and dine with him and he with me. (Rev. 3:20)

There was no room for Him in the inn at His birth, and there is still no room for Him in many hearts, the very ones for whom He died! This is so hard to understand. How can anyone refuse Him and such love? The good news is that He will continue to knock on the doors of those hearts so long as they are still beating. If your door is locked, please open to Him while there is yet time. It will change everything!

The Top of the Morning

Give the Lord the first of the day,
Arise early and seek;
He too will come without delay,
Eager to hear you speak…

The rest of the day will go well,
No matter comes what may;
Deposits of His love will swell,
His grace and mercy stay!

Oh, satisfy us early with Your mercy, that we may rejoice and be glad all our days! (Ps. 90:14)

My voice You shall hear in the morning, O Lord; in the morning I will direct it to You, and I will look up. (Ps. 5:3)

Sitting with the Lord first thing in the morning, just loving and listening, is a wonderful way to begin each day. Taking the time to turn the day over to Him can change our entire day—not so much the situations and difficulties that may arise but our reactions to those things. Most of us become so entangled in the affairs of life that we neglect making time with the Lord our first priority. As a result, stress and depression slip in. Give Him the first of each day. You will never regret it. Try it and see for yourself!

The Parables of the Fig Tree

> The branches already tender
> And putting forth their leaves;
> Satan soon forced to surrender,
> As Christ the world retrieves!
>
> Israel sees no fruit produced,
> Accepting its true King:
> Strangulation of the Law loosed,
> Eating grace's offering!

Now in the morning, as He returned to the city, He was hungry. And seeing a fig tree by the road, He came to it and found nothing on it but leaves, and said to it, "Let no fruit grow on you ever again." Immediately the fig tree withered away. (Matt. 21:18-19)

Now learn this parable from the fig tree: When its branch has already become tender and puts forth leaves, you know that summer is near. So you also, when you see all these things, you know it is near—at the doors! (Matt. 24:32-35)

This is about the parable of two fig trees—one producing no fruit, which Jesus cursed, and the second one about to yield its fruit. The first was an indictment of Israel under the Law of Moses, which produced no lasting fruit; the second was a sign of the Second Coming, the triumph of grace. Then Jew and Gentile (all who believe) will become "one man" in Christ and be filled with the Life and glory of Christ. First comes the Tribulation, then the Millennium or one thousand years of Christ's rule upon the earth, followed by a new heaven and new earth. Hallelujah!

Body and Head

*Christ must be both Body and Head
For Life to be released;
No independence, but instead
All self-assertion ceased…*

*Then the Spirit and the power
Of the Lord crucified
Can manifest, at the very hour
Self-reliance has died.*

> I am the vine, you are the branches. He who abides in Me, and I in him, bears much fruit; for without Me you can do nothing. If anyone does not abide in Me, he is cast out as a branch and is withered; and they gather them and throw them into the fire, and they are burned. If you abide in Me, and My words abide in you, you will ask what you desire, and it shall be done for you. By this My Father is glorified, that you bear much fruit; so you will be my disciples. (John 15:5-8)

The same life that is in the vine is in the branches, so the same Life that is in Christ is in each of His disciples—Life that must be released to do its work! Any time the soul gets involved in spiritual work (as its origin or power along the way) is like a branch trying to live severed from the vine; obviously, such a thing is impossible. But once the soul gets out of the way and only serves as steward to the spirit that draws its Life from the Spirit (Christ), victory over the enemy is certain, and bountiful fruit that lasts is produced, which in turn glorifies the Father. Nothing else works!

Proof of Love

The proof of love is to obey,
To do all Christ has said;
Following Him our chosen way,
The old man we were, dead…

And sacrificing the new one,
By His great love constrained;
Living out the Life of the Son,
Like Him, no more sin-stained…

If you love Me, keep My commandments. (John 14:15a)

For the love of Christ compels us. (2 Cor. 5:14a)

One proof of the love a man has for his wife is his faithfulness to his marital vows—forsaking all others and never guilty of infidelity or defiling the marital bed. The same is true if we truly love the Lord. We will keep His commandments and remain faithful in all things. If we do not, John 14:15a seems to indicate that we don't really love Him. And 2 Corinthians 5:14a says it even more strongly: His love for us and ours for Him compels or constrains us to remain faithful to all He has said. This is a most serious thing to consider.

The Ingredient of Glory

'Tis Christ alone we must access,
Only Him does God recognize;
Opens up the storehouse to bless
With all the Blood forever buys...

Nothing must be added to Christ,
No man-made idea or plan;
All required already sacrificed:
Priceless Life of Son of Man!

> Now the Lord is the Spirit; and where the Spirit of the Lord is, there is liberty. But we all, with unveiled face, beholding as in a mirror the glory of the Lord, are being transformed into the same image from glory to glory, just as by the Spirit of the Lord. (2 Cor. 3:17-18)

When Jesus said, "It is finished," He surely meant nothing else needed to be added to what He, the Spirit, and the Father had done. God's eternal purpose had been achieved. All would be as ordained, regardless of what the enemy or fallen man might do. Glory had been achieved, and that would never cease (from glory to glory forever, transforming us into the image of Christ).

We must neither add to nor take away from Christ's finished work. Again, hallelujah!

CRYING OUT FOR MORE

O Lord, open up the floodgate,
I need more than a taste;
My parched soul cries, "Inundate!"
Before I fall and waste

The glory of Your love and grace…
So hard in this stricken land,
Searching for my abiding place:
The oasis of Your hand!

> Blessed are those who hunger and thirst for righteousness, for they shall be filled. (Matt. 5:6)

I have been accused of never being satisfied and always wanting more of Christ. In some ways, that accusation is accurate. I am more than satisfied concerning my eternal fate and what Christ has done to accomplish that. But as I walk through this stricken land and survey the condition of my soul at any given moment, I cry out for more! I constantly need more of Him, and Matthew 5:6 seems to indicate that is completely normal. The enemy makes our pilgrimage from the earth to the Kingdom as difficult as possible, and we need more of Christ to make it through victoriously. So never stop hungering and thirsting. He will fill you every time you need it!

Abiding in Glory

> No way in glory to abide,
> Brilliance we could not bear;
> Full splendor must remain inside,
> Just fragments now to share…
>
> Greater release when glorified,
> Capacity then increased;
> Glory to glory multiplied,
> Ever-flowing, never ceased!

> If you abide in Me, and My words abide in you, you will ask what you desire, and it shall be done for you. By this My Father is glorified, that you bear much fruit; so you will be My disciples. (John 15:7-8)

Moses had to veil his face when he came down from the mountain, as the splendor of the glory of God was shining so brightly that others could not bear it. And yet we sing and pray that the glory would fall upon us, not knowing that if the fullness of His glory fell, we would be unable to bear it. So Christ in His mercy only releases what we can now tolerate. Once glorified at His appearing, we will be able to bear much more. But for now, we could never abide there. But what we are able to abide in is His Word and in Christ Himself. In fact, we must if we are to be His disciples, bear much fruit, and bring glory to the Father.

Hunger and Thirst

'Tis never enough, this foretaste,
My heart cries out for more!
I pledge to wait, abandon haste,
Linger, and still adore

No matter how long it may take:
Fill to its fullest my cup.
Your promise You cannot forsake…
I will open, we will sup!

I return once again to the topic of hungering and thirsting for more of Christ and His righteousness, nourishment we cannot do without. At times, the filling we crave and Christ's promises seems slow in coming. We may grow impatient and even desperate, but we must remember that no matter how long it may take, we will be fed. He has promised it, so we have His word on it. While waiting for the fulfillment of His word, do not grow weary and give up. Ask Him to grant you the word of His patience or perseverance (Rev. 3:10), and He will surely give it.

The Sedative of Comfort

Lord, the sedative of comfort
Has overtaken us;
Always to a bit more resort…
O God, awaken us!

Things are crumbling all around,
Yet pillows we adjust…
As long as such comforts abound,
No need in God to trust.

Because you say, "I am rich, have become wealthy, and have need of nothing—and do not know that you are wretched, miserable, poor, blind, and naked—I counsel you to buy from Me gold refined in the fire, that you may be rich; and white garments, that you may be clothed, that the shame of your nakedness may not be revealed; and anoint your eyes with eye salve, that you may see." (Rev. 3:17-18)

The situation at Laodicea is a picture of the church in America today. We have been so blessed by God with material blessings that we have become lukewarm toward the things of the Spirit, taking those blessings for granted and not seeing what has happened to us. The same malady infected Israel again and again, even taking them into exile in a foreign land. We desperately need the eye salve of the Spirit so that we might see our actual condition before it is too late and He "vomits" us out of His mouth!

Irresistible Grace*

The grace of God resistible,
Love of the Son refused?
Election, by reluctant will,
Overturned and abused?

In Christ before the foundation
Of heaven and the earth:
Secured by the Life of the Son,
Blood of infinite worth!

—*A doctrine of John Calvin

In Him also we have obtained an inheritance, being predestined according to the purpose of Him who works all things according to the counsel of His will, that we who first trusted in Christ should be to the praise of His glory. (Eph. 1:11-12)

And we know that all things work together for good to those who love God, to those who are the called according to His purpose. For whom He foreknew, He also predestined to be conformed to the image of His Son, that He might be the firstborn among brethren. Moreover whom He predestined, these He also called; whom He called, these He also justified; and whom He justified, these He also glorified. (Rom. 8:28-30)

Just as He chose us in Him before the foundation of the world, that we should be holy and without blame before Him in love, having predestined us

to adoption as sons by Jesus Christ to Himself.
(Eph. 1:4-5a)

These are very difficult passages to understand. By His foreknowledge, the Father chose those who are His and predestined them to be called, justified, and glorified. From such passages, John Calvin came up with the doctrine of irresistible grace, that those who belong to the Lord will eventually come to Him no matter what; that they may resist grace for a while but then will submit to it. I have no trouble with this because foreknowledge does not mean God caused some to believe and others not to believe; it simply means He, who knows all things, knew ahead of time who would believe in Christ and those who would not. Others may understand what is meant here differently, but it stands as truth, however understood.

Come!

"Come!" Christ says, "Lay down your heart."
He will fill it and heal;
Today is the best day to start,
Your heart no more conceal.

So many wounds over the years,
Buried so deep and hidden;
His grace will absorb all your tears
And thoroughly expunge all sin.

Come to Me, all you who labor and are heavy laden, and I will give you rest. Take my yoke upon you and learn from Me, for I am gentle and lowly in heart, and you will find rest for your souls. For My yoke is easy and My burden is light. (Matt. 11:28-30)

And the Spirit and bride say, "Come!" And let him who hears say, "Come!" And let him who thirsts come. Whoever desires, let him take the water of life freely. (Rev. 22:17)

Jesus told us that in this world we will have tribulation, for the world in its current condition is the product of Satan and fallen man. But because He has overcome the world, He also invited us to come to Him for rest and healing. By giving our burdens and sorrows to Him, we receive in their place rest—rest in Him, knowing that the way to the victory which He has won is by surrendering our very lives to Him. The battle is the Lord's, not ours, and He has already won!

The Purpose of Deserts

Praise You for this desert again,
What new things am I to see?
When will the revelations begin,
How long must I stay thirsty?

Return me by Your heat refined,
More flesh burned out and gone;
Remake me by pattern designed
And ordained at Eden's dawn…

And we know that all things work together for good to those who love God, to those who are called according to His purpose. (Rom. 8:28)

And you shall remember that the Lord your God led you all the way these forty years in the wilderness, *to humble you and test you to know what was in your heart, whether you would keep His commandments or not.* (Deut. 8:2, emphasis mine)

Then Jesus was led up by the Spirit into the wilderness to be tempted by the devil. (Matt. 4:1)

Desert experiences in the Spirit are times of testing to see if what we have learned from the Lord has become part of our makeup and growth, or things that hardship and suffering will undo. Such times are needed to humble us and to teach us not to depend upon ourselves but upon the Spirit of Christ. The flesh (our mind, will, and emotions included) cannot prevail in spiritual battles (John 3:6). Only the Life of Christ released through our submission to Him can come out victorious.

Full Value

Consume us completely, O Lord,
We are Your burning ones!
To Eden's pure plan be restored,
Reap the fruit of Your Son's

Perfect Life and great sacrifice…
For You the full value
Of such an exorbitant price:
All of us, all of You!

He must increase, but I must decrease. (John 3:30)

And He is the head of the body, the church, who is the beginning, the firstborn from the dead, that in all things He may *have the preeminence.* (Col. 1:18, emphasis mine)

Blessed are those who keep His testimonies, who seek Him with the whole heart. (Ps. 119:2)

For without Me you can do nothing. (John 15:5b)

It takes the whole heart given to Christ to receive His full blessings; anything less yields a diminished return or yield. The wise virgins of Matthew 25 were those who gave all of themselves to the Lord, holding nothing back. The foolish virgins, on the other hand, were unwilling to yield everything; certain things they just could not give over. As a result, they were not allowed entrance to the

Wedding Supper of the Lamb; but the wise ones were allowed in to celebrate with the Lord, being part of the Bride. Jesus held nothing back; He gave His all and calls us to do the same for Him. How can any of us say no to such love and sacrifice?

Exploring the Kingdom 2

So much in the Kingdom to explore,
Largely uncharted land;
Few pilgrims have been there before,
Though forever planned…

The Lord Jesus Christ the King there,
His rule is absolute;
If His glory we hope to share,
No Word can we dispute.

In those days John the Baptist came preaching in the wilderness of Judea, and saying, "Repent, for the kingdom is at hand." (Matt. 3:1-2)

But if I cast out demons by the Spirit of God, surely the kingdom of God has come upon you. (Matt. 12:28-29)

Many have discerned that the Kingdom of God is the central meaning of the coming and ministry of Jesus, the very essence of His message. And yet few agree on just what the Kingdom of God is. There will be some point in the future when Satan is bound in a bottomless pit for a thousand years and Christ reigns. And that is certainly true. Others think the Kingdom of God is already present and has been since our Messiah entered the world over two thousand years ago. The Kingdom will certainly be an actual place, a realm where Christ rules and reigns. But it is also a state of being, in the heart of those who already submit to the rulership of

Christ. The Kingdom is any place and at any time where Christ rules—both a present reality and a future realm. With Satan bound, the glory of the Kingdom will be incredible in its manifestation!

The Smallest Things

On the smallest things, life revolves,
Of the great, their foundation;
Following through on small resolves
Crux of Kingdom's creation!

'Tis the day in, day out habits,
Repeated and repeated,
Prize of the overcomer gets…
And next to the Lord seated!

His lord said to him, "Well done, good and faithful servant; you were faithful over a few things, I will make you ruler over many things. Enter into the joy of your lord." (Matt. 25:21)

For who has despised the day of small things? (Zech. 4:10a)

We must be faithful in the smallest of things if we are ever to attain to greater ones. Our life of faith begins with simple obedience to the things we understand, and we are only given bigger ones when we have proven ourselves faithful and obedient in the small ones. Mother Teresa was once asked how she could ever have taken on such a seemingly impossible task for God, one with little chance for success. Her answer? "God has not called me to succeed, but rather to be faithful." Wherever you are with God, tending to basic things or to much more complex ones, let that be your approach as well—faithfulness—for that is all He expects from you.

The Purpose of Pain

The Spirit never wastes our pain…
He will turn it to good
If our trust in Him we maintain,
Whether it's understood

Or comprehension is slow to come;
Never for its own sake:
It prepares us for the Kingdom,
And more like Christ will make…

And lest I should be exalted above measure by the abundance of the revelations, a thorn in the flesh was given to me, a messenger of Satan to buffet me, lest I be exalted above measure…Therefore I take pleasure in infirmities, in reproaches, in needs, in persecutions, in distresses, for Christ's sake. For when I am weak, then I am strong. (2 Cor. 12:7, 10)

For I consider that the sufferings of this present time are not worthy to be compared with the glory which shall be revealed in us. (Rom. 8:18)

All of us suffer in this life, whether we are believers in Christ or not. But for those who believe, that suffering is not for its own sake or in vain. It refines us, making us more like our Savior. And it drives us to Him, the only place we can find relief and some understanding of what we are going through. Our enemy does anything the Lord God allows in an effort to thwart the building of the Kingdom. For when it comes, he and his kingdom are finished! So stand fast and do not be moved!

The Goodness of God

Once you have tasted the goodness
And the grace of the King,
You will never settle for less,
Nor desire anything

Except He who alone sustains,
Who points the homeward way…
Finest of the wine and choice grains
Gives as journey's mainstay!

Oh, taste and see that the Lord is good; blessed is the man who trusts him Him! (Ps. 34:8)

Therefore, laying aside all malice, all deceit, hypocrisy, and all evil speaking, as newborn babes, desire the pure milk of the word, that you grow thereby, if indeed you have tasted that the Lord is gracious. (1 Pet. 2:1-3)

The best of all first fruits of any kind…shall be the priest's. (Ezek. 44:30a)

Once the Lord has graciously given us even a small sampling of His goodness, we find ourselves wanting more! In fact, the things that the world offers no longer satisfy, and we gradually give up pursuing anything but God. This is difficult to understand for one who has never experienced it; only a taste of the real thing will ever convince them otherwise. But once they do, they too will be hooked!

~ Rod Connell

Immovable

Rock of our salvation will not move,
Love cannot be undone;
Father poured out Spirit to prove
The triumph of His Son!

Now the battle is up to us,
His power to access;
As immovable as Jesus...
This alone will God bless!

Jesus Christ is the same yesterday, today, and forever. (Heb. 13:8)

For I am the Lord, I do not change. (Mal. 3:6)

The love of God is the only immutable thing in the universe. It is unbreakable and immovable— the very definition of who He is. And it is that same power, in Christ and in us, that we must allow to live. For when His Life comes forth, it expresses itself in the power of His love, and Satan is left defenseless and defeated before such an opponent. The only deterrent to that victory is us, the fleshly nature of our soul (our mind, will, and emotions). We must learn to lay that aside and live by the Spirit alone, releasing His love.

The Law of the Son

By the Spirit of Life set free,
A higher law in place;
From both sin and death, liberty!
The chains unlocked by grace...

But its purpose we must set free:
Only by submission
Do we see its supremacy...
Perfect law of the Son!

For the law of the Spirit of life in Christ Jesus has made me free from the law of sin and death. (Rom. 8:2)

Bear one another's burdens, and so fulfill the law of Christ. (Gal. 6:2)

The law of sin and death, operational since the Garden, has been overcome by the law of the Spirit of life in Christ Jesus; for the only thing that can overcome a law is a higher law. For all believers, that law is within, the very way the Life of Christ manifests itself. It is a law that operates by love for God, for self, and for others. All the divine virtues that Jesus taught are found in the expression of that Life and love. The only requirement on our part is submission and death of self (the old man) so that the new man in Christ can come forth. Any other method is a way of the flesh.

From the Scales to Rest

The scales so hard to throw away
And learn in Christ to rest:
Oft it is those who go astray
Who seem most highly blessed...

Still, we must continue to be
Expressions of our Lord;
To trust in Him implicitly...
Sure to come His reward!

Then the Lord took the man and put him in the garden of Eden to tend and keep it. And the Lord God commanded the man, saying, "Of every tree of the garden you may freely eat; but of the tree of the knowledge of good and evil you shall not eat, for in the day that you eat of it you shall surely die. (Gen. 2:15-17)

Why do you look on those who deal treacherously, and hold Your tongue when the wicked devours a person more righteous than he? (Hab. 1:13b)

The fallen world, since the Garden of Eden, has operated by what I call the scales: two sides to everything: good and evil, positive and negative; an either-or way of thinking. So when we try on our own to live "good" as the world defines it, we expect to be rewarded on the other end of scales: one side goes down, and the other should come up. (Do you get the picture?) But the good as God defines it does not always produce that result. In fact, things may even get worse, which makes it difficult to understand. Habakkuk points that out very clearly in his complaint to God. Another way of saying it—and someone wrote about it—is, Why do bad things happen to good people? Christ told us we would suffer tribulation under such a system, but He tells us to be of good cheer nonetheless. He has overcome the world and its perverse systems, so we must have faith that when He returns, all things will be made right.

The Danger of Distractions

The old master of distractions,
Our focus to deflect,
Offers up sweet satisfactions
Designed to disconnect...

Anything to avert our eyes,
From Christ to look away;
Too distracted to realize
How far from Him we stray.

Therefore, when your eye is good ["single" in other translations], your whole body also is full of light. (Luke 11:34a)

And this I say for your own profit, not that I may put a leash on you, but for what is proper, and that you may serve the Lord without distraction. (1 Cor. 7:35)

Therefore we also, since we are surrounded by so great a cloud of witnesses, let us lay aside every weight, and the sin which so easily ensnares us, and let us run with endurance the race that is set before us, looking unto Jesus ["fixing our eyes upon" in NIV], the author and finisher of our faith, who for the joy that was set before Him endured the cross, despising the shame, and has sat down at the right hand of the throne of God. (Heb. 12:1-2)

We must keep our eyes and heart on Christ and His goal of perfecting us and building the Kingdom. Satan tries everything he can to ensnare us: old sins and temptations, illness, family problems, financial difficulties, etc. And we can be drawn into too much comfort, too many hours watching television, too many material blessings—the list goes on and on. So we must be vigilant over our time and efforts, putting God first and everything else second at best!

The Mind of Christ

It takes the mind of Christ to discern
The light the Spirit sends;
Only by His can we hear and learn
Truth that our mind transcends…

To the natural, foolishness,
Too dull mere intellect;
But His own mind He gave to bless,
To strengthen and direct!

And do not be conformed to this world, but be transformed by the renewing of your mind, that you may prove what is that good and acceptable and perfect will of God. (Rom. 12:2)

For "who has known the mind of the Lord that he may instruct him?" But we have the mind of Christ. (1 Cor. 2:16)

We only have the benefit of the mind of Christ if we allow Him to be the Head, letting Him make the decisions and giving us divine understanding. Our own mind must continually be renewed, for old ways of thinking hang on long after our salvation experience (Rom. 12:2; Eph. 4:23). Our faith must overcome our fallen reason, a faculty much esteemed by fallen man but one that is limited and fallible. Only what God says is not, and His ways of thinking come to us by the mind of Christ.

The Rewards of Patience

It is so hard to sit and wait,
Hearing not a word;
But if impatience we delay,
Crucial what is heard…

Our own plans stopped, overturned,
Spirit's choice instead;
In those few moments may be heard
Wisdom from the Head!

Be still, and know that I am God. (Ps. 46:10)

But those who wait on the Lord shall renew their strength; they shall mount up with wings like eagles, they shall run and not be weary, they shall walk and not faint. (Isa. 40:31)

My brethren, count it all joy when you fall into various trials, knowing that the testing of your faith produces patience. But let patience have its perfect work, that you may be perfect and complete, lacking nothing. (James 1:2-4)

Patience is not a virtue of fallen man—he wants what he wants, and he wants it right now! It takes faith in Christ and His indwelling Spirit to have true patience. "Patience" is sometimes translated as "perseverance" in Scripture, and it certainly takes divine patience to persevere in the face of adversity. We all must learn to just sit before God and be still so that we might receive His strength to remain patient despite the most trying circumstances. If we do not, it is likely that we will respond in the flesh, which may solve some problem temporarily. But God promises to bless those who are patient before Him, and His solutions are permanent!

Ushers of the Kingdom

Overcomers, the willing hearts
Long before prophesied,
Emerging in greater numbers,
Soon will turn the tide!

Those who have made Christ all in all,
On Him fully depend...
The consequences of the Fall
Finally at an end!

Your people shall be volunteers [willing hearts] in the day of Your power; in the beauties of holiness, from the womb of the morning, You have the dew of Your youth. (Ps. 110:3)

Therefore, since all these things will be dissolved, what manner of persons ought you to be in holy conduct and godliness, looking for and *hastening the coming of the day God*. (2 Pet. 4:11-12a)

The first time I realized that I (and you) have anything to do with the coming of the Lord and in hastening His coming, I was overwhelmed. What a responsibility! I also realized that if we can hasten His return, we can also slow it down and delay it. In fact, that has been one of the main strategies of Satan since Calvary: to work through us so as to delay the inevitable return of Christ. He has done it in a variety of ways: false teaching, diminishing the true gospel, and causing division and weakness. He has appealed to the soul of man, which is part of the flesh, knowing that soulish efforts only result in failure to produce true and lasting fruit, thereby prolonging his stay as the prince of this world. But the Spirit of the Lord has awakened some to this ploy, and they are willing to do anything to hasten the coming of the King, not loving their own lives even unto death, whether physical or spiritual! Hallelujah! Even so, come quickly, Lord Jesus!

Springs of Glory

On world and flesh the doom of thirst,
Never getting their fill;
Only when we put the Lord first,
Drink of His perfect will,

Do we find we thirst no more
For what's but transitory;
For in Him alone the full store
Of satisfying glory!

Jesus answered and said to her, "If you knew the gift of God, and who it is who says to you, 'Give Me a drink,' you would have asked Him, and He would have given you living water…Whoever drinks of this water will thirst again, but whoever drinks of the water that I shall give him will never thirst. But the water that I shall give him will become to him a fountain of water springing up into everlasting life." (John 4:10, 13)

But we all with unveiled face, beholding as in a mirror the glory of the Lord, are being transformed into the same image from glory to glory, just as by the Spirit of the Lord. (2 Cor. 3:18)

The problem with worldly pleasures is that they never fully satisfy; they only temporarily pacify us. But we are always left with a thirst for more, only to find the same result when we indulge again. The pleasures of sin are for but a season, leaving disillusionment and even destruction in their wake. But drinking living water from its source completely satisfies and eliminates hunger and thirst for anything else. "From glory to glory," the Scripture puts it. Come, take a drink and see!

Seed Moments

All those seed moments I cherish,
The plantings of the Lord;
From them spring Life, never to perish,
Jesus Himself the guard!

To guard and to carefully attend,
Water and cultivate;
In due time precious fruit will send,
Riches of His estate!

But Jesus answered them, saying, "The hour has come that the Son Man should be glorified. Most assuredly, I say to you, unless a grain of wheat falls into the ground and dies, it remains alone, but if it dies, it produces much grain. He who love his life will lose it, and he who hates his life in this world will keep it for eternal life. If anyone serves Me, let him follow Me, and where I am, there My servant will be also. If anyone serves Me, him My Father will honor." (John 12:23-26)

But others fell on good ground and yielded a crop; some a hundred-fold, some sixty, some thirty. He who has ears to hear, let him hear! (Matt. 13:8)

Once the Spirit has prepared the soil of the heart and "good ground" appears, Christ can plant the seed of His Word and be assured of a bountiful crop. But it requires much in the way of disciplining the flesh: removing stony places and weeds, plowing, cultivation, and just the right amount of revelation (light) and the living water of life—all in due season. To this we must be willing to submit if we truly desire to produce lasting fruit for the Lord.

Firsthandedness

There must be a firsthandedness,
Directly to us from Christ;
Less than that can a moment bless
And temporarily suffice…

But it takes Him and Him alone
A lasting change to make;
Only His Life, become our own,
Foe unable to break.

For there is one God and one Mediator between God and men, the Man Christ Jesus, who gave Himself a ransom for all, to be testified in due time. (2 Tim. 2:3a)

Teaching and correct doctrine are good things, but they must not be overemphasized to the point of hindering the Life of Christ from coming forth. Rather, they must point us to the Life so that we come to trust in it and Him alone. Truth is not something to copy and try to achieve; it is Christ! When He comes forth and manifests, all is made right. But if He does not, a cheap imitation is all that will ever be produced.

Play Those Harps!

Harps on a weeping willow tree
No songs of praise can make;
Pray the Spirit will help you see
Dark moods a grave mistake…

Instead, use attacks as means to grow,
Made stronger by resistance;
Prove futile all schemes of the foe—
Play those harps…sing and dance!

By the rivers of Babylon, there we sat down, yea, we wept when we remembered Zion. We hung our harps upon the willows in the midst of it. For there those who carried us away captive asked of us a song, and those who plundered us requested mirth, saying, "Sing us one of the songs of Zion." How shall we sing the Lord's song in a foreign land? (Ps. 137:1-4)

Praise the Lord! Sing to the Lord a new song, and His praise in the assembly of the saints. Let Israel rejoice in their Maker; let the children of Zion be joyful in their King. Let them praise His name with the dance; let them sing praises to Him with the timbrel and harp. For the Lord takes pleasure in His people; He will beautify the humble with salvation. (Ps. 149:1-4)

In captivity, under the law, only sadness and longing prevailed. Harps were hung silently on willow trees, and gloom was the prevailing mood of the people. They could find no reason to sing and celebrate. Today, we are still in a world that mocks us, asking such questions as "Where is your God?" (Ps. 42:3) Evil seems to be winning as we survey the things around us. And yet, we can sing, dance and celebrate! For we know our redemption draws nigh, that our Redeemer lives! Hallelujah! Soon, very soon now, His grace will prevail.

From Faith to Faith

After conversion, cloudless skies
And unabated sun!
But soon, of course, changes arise,
And fair weather is done...

Path of faith meets new turbulence,
To new levels must rise;
Become strong by wind's resistance,
Steadfast despite skies...

For I am not ashamed of the gospel of Christ, for it is the power of God to salvation for everyone who believes, for the Jew first and also for the Greek. For in it the righteousness of God is revealed from faith to faith; as it is written, "The just shall by faith." (Rom. 1:16-17)

My brethren, count it all joy when you fall into various trials. (James 1:2)

Faith cannot grow without testing and resistance. Therefore, the Lord allows us to fall into "various trials," as James puts it. When we are first saved, we seem to be in a protective bubble for a while—the grace of the Lord, which allows our newly born faith to take root. But in due time, the protection is removed (or partially at least), and the enemy attacks in an effort to steal, kill, and destroy. He means it unto evil but the Father means unto good (Gen. 50:20) to bring us to full maturity in the Lord and to rid us of any self-dependence that remains. We must become fully submitted and dependent on Him alone, our soul divided from our spirit.

Christ Unveiled

Out of our boxes, Christ release,
Too long He's been confined!
It is time for us to decrease,
His glory no more bind…

Time to be desperate, broken,
To see why we have failed;
Truly hear all He has spoken,
His face no longer veiled!

He must increase, but I must decrease. (John 3:30)

And why do we stand in jeopardy every hour? I affirm, by the boasting in you which I have in Christ Jesus our Lord, I die daily. (1 Cor. 15:30-31)

Only in brokenness are we made whole. So the Spirit allows us to fail again and again in our walk with Christ until we come to see the reason for our failures and frustration. When we finally grasp this revelation, the Life of Christ is released to do the work we could not do. Jacob struggled with this for years before his wrestling match with the preincarnate Christ at Peniel. As a result, his hip was separated from its socket, and he was left with a limp for the rest of his life. But he was also a changed man. He realized that it must be God that he should depend upon in all circumstances and not himself. Paul also came to this revelation and lived accordingly, "dying daily" to self.

~ Rod Connell

JESUS KNOWS

I press to my lips a passage
Speaking to my travails;
Those promises soothe and massage,
Their relief never fails

So grateful Christ came as a man
And knows just how we feel;
Integral part of Father's plan
His humanity to reveal...

Seeing then that we have a great High Priest who has passed through the heavens, Jesus the Son of God, let us hold fast our confession. For we do not have a High Priest who cannot sympathize with our weaknesses, but was in all points tempted as we are, yet without sin. Let us therefore come boldly to the throne of grace, that we may obtain mercy and find grace to help in time of need. (Heb. 4:14-16)

For every trial in life, God has given us a promise. We must never forget that no matter how harsh a hardship might be. Of course, we must know the Word to know what those promises are! So many believers depend upon teachers of the Word, but they are not reading and meditating on it much themselves. I am going through yet another attack from the enemy right now, and it drove me to the Word to remind me that God is always faithful. I am lacking wisdom at the moment, so I am asking God to grant me His wisdom. He promises to give it liberally and without reproach, so I am waiting for Him to give it. And I am praying that my faith has no double-mindedness in it, that I fully believe He will answer soon. Remember this the next time you are facing the attacks of our foe. Go to His promises!

~ Rod Connell

Looking Ahead

In Your presence, fullness of joy!
Nothing the foe can do...
A sweetness that does not cloy,
Immersed in all that's true:

Shadows and the false fall away,
As the glory increases...
O Lord, how I long here to stay,
Where all conflict ceases!

> You will show me the path of life; in Your presence is fullness of joy; at Your right hand are pleasures forevermore. (Ps. 16:11)

Ephesians 2:4-7 tells us that in Christ Jesus, we are already seated in "heavenly places." Did you get that? Right now, if you are a believer, you are seated with Jesus, who is at the right hand of the Father! That is your present position, but the enemy does everything in his power to keep you ignorant of that fact or to cause you to forget it and act from the flesh. When you are struggling, remind yourself and Satan where you are: in Christ's very presence, looking down on all the activities of darkness. Remember to keep that heavenly perspective and altitude, and Satan has to flee!

Pressing On

The closer to God, more the attacks,
For a danger to the foe;
If pursuit slows and we relax,
False sense of peace we know...

Nevertheless, we must not relent,
But persevere, press on;
To build the Kingdom we are sent,
Not let up till foe is gone!

My brethren, count it all joy when you fall into various trials, knowing that the testing of your faith produces patience. But let patience have its perfect work, that you may be perfect and complete, lacking nothing. (James 1:2-4)

Because you have kept My command to persevere, I also will keep you from the hour of trial which shall come upon the whole world. (Rev. 3:10)

Satan knows he has lost. He was already defeated by Christ on Calvary and given the sentence of being bound in the bottomless pit for a thousand years, followed by the lake of fire for eternity. All he can do is prolong his stay as the prince of this world and delay the execution of his sentence. Anyone working to build the Kingdom of God is the target of his worst attacks, for they threaten his very existence on earth and shorten the time he is allowed to stay in power. All the more reason to dig in and not be moved by his buffeting! Are you willing to volunteer for this campaign?

Bone and Marrow

The spirit of man the marrow,
The soul is but the bone;
Spirit the way straight and narrow,
Direct line to the throne…

A steward the soul is to be,
To listen and obey;
Only spirit can Spirit see,
Hear what He has to say…

> For the word of God is living and powerful, and sharper than any two-edged sword, piercing even to the division of soul and spirit, and of joints and marrow, and is a discerner of the thoughts and intents of the heart. (Heb. 4:12)

So many believers do not know that they are three-part beings—spirit, soul, and body. They either have not thought about it or they believe soul and spirit are one and the same, two names for one part of their makeup. Hebrews 4:12 says otherwise and declares that these two parts must be separated and allowed to function as God intended at creation: the spirit to communicate with His Spirit, the soul to be the steward of the spirit, and the body to carry out what the spirit has received from the Spirit of God. The verse of 1 Thessalonians 5:24 makes this distinction as well: "Now may the God of peace Himself sanctify you completely; and may *your whole spirit, soul, and body* be preserved blameless at the coming of our Lord Jesus Christ. He who calls you is faithful, who also will do it" (emphasis mine). This is so critical to understand if we are to make any real spiritual progress!

Patience

In patience your soul you possess,
Grounded in hope and trust;
Great treasures are waiting to bless,
But patience is a must!

Father will always keep His word,
Whether early or late;
So store away promise you heard,
Then worship as you wait!

By your patience possess your soul. (Luke 21:19)

Behold, I have refined you, but not as silver; I have tested you in the furnace of affliction. (Isa. 48:10)

We seem again to be on the subject of suffering and undergoing trials for the Lord. This will be a continual battle until Christ returns. If you have not gone through much of this yet, you will, especially the more sold out you are to Christ. But when you do, remember this promise: the peace that passes understanding (Phil. 4:6-7) is yours if you will just reach out and take it!
    Believe God and let your patience and faith be tested until you are perfect and complete, "lacking nothing" (James 1:4).

Lest We Forget

Since this world is not His Kingdom,
How can we claim it ours?
We are each here as a pilgrim,
Passing faithful hours

Awaiting the King's soon return;
'Tis so easy to forget,
For earthly trifles to yearn…
And fickle hearts to fret!

Jesus answered, "My kingdom is not of this world…but now My kingdom is not from here. (John 18:36)

By faith Abraham obeyed when he was called to go out to the place which he would receive as an inheritance. And he went out, not knowing where he was going. By faith he dwelt in the land of promise as in a foreign country…for he waited for the city which has foundations, whose builder and maker is God. (Heb. 11:8, 10)

The world has a way of drawing us in to become an active part of it—not in its sin and darkness but into its day-to-day distractions and problems. We must be a part of it in order to spread the gospel and build the Kingdom, but the danger is getting so drawn in that we neglect the work of the Lord and our own spiritual progress. If the Lord's Kingdom is not of this world, we must not allow it to be ours either! Do not get so entangled in the affairs of this world. Remember who you are and how you are to live while here. And stay busy about your Father's affairs!

His Presence

His presence is what I live for,
To know that He is near;
When troubles hit and I need more,
Even His whisper hear!

When I sense He is far away,
Dry is my soul and cold;
But drink and heat return to stay
When He returns to hold!

Draw near to God and He will draw near to you. (James 4:8a)

Why are you cast down, O my soul? And why are you disquieted within me? Hope in God, for I shall yet praise Him for the help of His countenance. (Ps. 42:5)

Blessed are those who hunger and thirst for righteousness, for they shall be filled. (Matt. 5:6)

Oh, for the day when we will be in His presence continually—when the enemy, darkness, and all distractions are no longer part of life! In the meanwhile, we must stay attuned to His presence on a spiritual plane for He promised to be with us always and to never leave nor forsake us. Daily prayer and surrender to His will and daily Bible reading are great reminders of that glorious fact!

~ Rod Connell

Artificial Fruit

Without the seed there is no root,
Nothing to earth to cling;
Without the root there is no fruit,
Only a lifeless thing…

Faith without repentance is dead,
No new Life is produced;
Man's artificial fruit instead,
By *do's* and *don'ts* infused.

In those days John the Baptist came preaching in the wilderness of Judea, and saying, "Repent, for the kingdom of heaven is at hand." (Matt. 3:1-2)

From that time, Jesus began to preach and to say, "Repent, for the kingdom of heaven is at hand." (Matt. 4:17)

Now after John was put in prison, Jesus came to Galilee, preaching the gospel of the kingdom, and saying, "The time is fulfilled, and the kingdom of God is at hand. Repent and believe in the gospel." (Mark 1:15)

Without true repentance and faith, salvation cannot be gained—only a counterfeit version that can only produce artificial fruit. Repentance means more than simply being sorry for sin; it means deep godly sorrow and turning from it. True belief in the sacrificial death of Christ includes both faith and repentance. Satan has worked hard to eliminate the need for repentance in the process of salvation, knowing that it is absolutely necessary for any real change to take place. Beware if you have come to believe his lie!

The Poor in Spirit

Are you poor enough to receive?
He only gives to these…
Are you poor enough to believe?
Then come, take what you please!

The greatest gifts offered to man,
But only to the poor;
For the rich in spirit, no plan…
They have no need of more!

> Blessed are the poor in spirit, for theirs is the kingdom of heaven. (Matt. 5:3)

There has been much discussion over just what Jesus meant by the phrase "the poor in spirit." Certainly much of His preaching and ministering was to the materially poor, those who had no one to turn to except God. When one reaches that state, he has become truly dependent and open to receive the needed help. But there is also another meaning: poor in spirit can be seen in contrast to those who consider themselves rich in spirit, like the believers at Laodicea, who were actually spiritually destitute and did not know it. All of us are poor in spirit, whether we know it or not. The ones who do know it will reach out to God, and He has promised them the Kingdom of heaven. Those who do not know it will remain lost in their pride.

A Return to Intimacy

Lifted forever is the veil
Hiding the divine face;
Access now even though we fail,
God's incredible grace!

Human effort would never do,
So Father sent His Son;
Making a way for me and you,
Eden intimacy won!

Then, behold, the veil of the temple was torn in two from top to bottom; and the earth quaked, and the rocks were split, and the graves were opened; and many bodies of the saints who had fallen asleep were raised. (Matt. 27:51)

Therefore, brethren, having boldness to enter the Holiest by the blood of Jesus, by a new and living way which He consecrated for us, through the veil, that is, His flesh, and having a High Priest over the house of God, let us draw near with a true heart in full assurance of faith, having our hearts sprinkled from an evil conscience and our bodies washed with pure water. (Heb. 10:19-22)

In the Garden of Eden, Adam and Eve had full access to God, walking and talking to Him. But once sin entered, that intimacy was lost, and they were cast out of God's presence. That separation is what the veil in the temple was all about, the barrier between God and man. Hebrews 10 even calls the veil "the flesh of Christ."

So when His flesh was torn and destroyed, the veil was also ripped, giving mankind entrance into the holiest and intimacy with God once again! Enter in often and commune with Him. The only thing better than that is when we shall see Him face to face!

At Hand

Repent, the Kingdom is at hand,
God reached more than halfway!
He became a man, sent to stand
Among men who go astray…

His hand there yet, still extended,
For all who will take hold;
A firm grasp and curse is ended,
Kingdom soon to unfold!

For God so loved the world that He gave His only begotten Son, that whoever believes in Him should not perish but have everlasting life. (John 3:16)

Let this mind be in you which was also in Christ Jesus, who, being in the form of God, did not consider it robbery to be equal with God, but made Himself of no reputation, taking the form of a bondservant, and coming in the likeness of men. (Phil. 2:5-7)

When John the Baptist declared that the Kingdom was at hand, it had come because the King had come! And where He is, for those who submit to His Kingship, the Kingdom indeed has already come! He became a man, one of us, and overcame Satan, sin, and death. His hand of salvation is extended to all who will reach out and take it. And some day soon, He will return materially and establish His Kingdom here on earth, not only spiritually but physically as well! Praise You, Lord!

~ Rod Connell

Two Songs to Sing

Sing the song of deliverance,
Sing of eternal care;
With Moses sing the first and dance,
With Christ the second share…

The song of Moses and the Lamb,
Freed from both law and sin;
Celebrate with the great I-AM,
Two songs that never end!

And I saw something like a sea of glass mingled with fire, and those who have victory over the beast, over his image and over his mark and over the number of his name, standing on the sea of glass, having harps of God. They sing the song of Moses, the servant of God, and the song of the Lamb, saying, "Great and marvelous are Your works, Lord God Almighty! Just and true are Your ways, O King of the saints! Who shall not fear You, O Lord, and glorify Your name? For You alone are holy. For all nations shall come and worship before You, for Your judgments have been manifested." (Rev. 15:2-4)

In Exodus 15, Moses and Miriam sang a song of celebration, celebrating their deliverance from Egypt and the hand of pharaoh. It was a song of high praise and jubilation. Moses sang again in Deuteronomy 32, just before he was "taken" by the Lord and not allowed to enter the land of promise. This second is a reminder to all the people of the Lord's excellent greatness, things they were never to forget once Moses was gone. What a man! Singing even though he was not going over to enjoy the fruits of his labor! And then, of course, the song of the Lamb mentioned in Revelation 15, sung by those who had not taken the mark of the beast during the Great Tribulation. The song of Moses will also be sung then, both songs a great praise and celebration of the mercy, grace, and love of God!

Oh, the Blood!

The Blood of both God and man
Dripping down a cruel cross;
Foe thought he had spoiled the plan,
But for him eternal loss!

Sin and death are now defeated,
For our King we await;
Next to Him soon to be seated,
Never to leave Kingdom's gate!

Then I heard a loud voice saying in heaven, "Now salvation, and strength, and the kingdom of our God, and the power of His Christ have come, for the accuser of the brethren, who accused them before our God day and night, has been cast down. And they overcame by the blood of the Lamb and the word of their testimony, and they did not love their lives to the death. (Rev. 12:10-11)

Satan's grand gambit was the death of Christ on the Cross. Indeed, he was sure this would be his path to victory. But in the end it was a foolish move, for it played directly into the Father's hands and plans, the very move needed to ensure the success of the divine goal, the salvation of man and the coming of the Kingdom! So we now wait for the next step, the return of the King and His millennial reign. Lord, we praise you for the Blood and for those who "did not love their lives to the death." Maranatha!

The Shade of the Cross

Going through where we all must go,
But with grace and a song!
Jesus came so that He might know
Trials that to flesh belong…

He passed them all with such grace
He made for us a way:
No matter what hardships you face,
In shade of the Cross stay!

> He who dwells in the secret place of the Most High shall abide under the shadow of the Almighty. I will say to the Lord, "He is my refuge and my fortress; My God, in Him, I will trust…Because he has set his love upon Me, therefore I will deliver him; I will set him on high, because he has known My name. He shall call upon Me, and I will answer him; I will be with him in trouble; I will deliver him and honor him. With long life I will satisfy him, and show him my salvation." (Ps. 91:1-2, 14-16)

The shadow and the shade cast by the Cross is the "secret place of the Most High." It is a place of safety, a refuge, the one place we cannot be defeated! For all those who love Him more than even their own lives, this is where they abide. And because they love the Lord that much, all His promises become theirs. These He will deliver out of trouble. He will deliver and honor them. He will grant them long life and show them all the dimensions of His marvelous salvation!

Working from Victory

Not working to victory but from—
Christ has already won!
Now preparing for the Kingdom,
Ready to meet the Son!

Oh, what a song we have to sing,
As in His bosom we rest!
Spoils of war of our great King
He gives to all His blessed!

So when Jesus had received the sour wine, He said, "It is finished!" And bowing His head, He gave up His spirit. (John 19:30)

Yet in all these things we are more than conquerors, through Him who loved us. For I am persuaded that neither death nor life, nor angels nor principalities nor powers, nor things present nor things to come, nor height nor depth, nor any other created thing, shall be able to separate us from the love of God which is in Christ Jesus our Lord. (Rom. 8:37-39)

These things I have spoken to you, that in Me you may have peace. In this world you will have tribulation; but be of good cheer; I have overcome the world. (John 16:33)

We must always remember that Christ has already won. He has gone ahead of us, defeating the enemy and preparing a way for us to win as well. Nothing can keep that from becoming a reality. The problem is that we sometimes forget it, and when the attacks get extremely fierce, we try to fight the battle in our own power. The battle is the Lord's, and Satan must be reminded of that eternal fact. Resist him in this way and he has to flee. It is finished. All that God has ordained will come to pass!

Ever Becoming

Becoming but never to arrive,
Essence of all finite;
Spark of eternally alive,
God has done it just right!

'Tis enough to be like the Lord,
Ever closer, yet not quite;
Always another step upward,
Always a bit more light!

Always learning and never able to come to the knowledge of the truth. (2 Tim. 3:7)

When I was a child, I spoke as a child, I understood as a child. I thought as a child; but when I became a man, I put away childish things. For now we see in a mirror, dimly, but then face to face. Now I know in part, but then I shall know just as I also am known. (Rom. 13:11-12)

Natural man is ever learning but never able to come to the truth in Jesus Christ. It takes a spiritual awakening and a new man for that to happen. But even after salvation and on into eternity, we will never come to the end of the knowledge and glory of Christ. We shall be like Him and know Him as He is, which is infinite! Every new day will bring some new aspect of who He is in all His glory, and that will never end. Wow!

What Christ Is Looking For

A place where Jesus feels at home,
Like He did in Bethany;
A place where He can be Himself,
In divine simplicity...

Where He is fed and freely feeds,
Close friend as well as Lord;
Mutual fulfilling of needs,
And mutually adored!

And Jesus went into Jerusalem and into the temple. So when He had looked around at all things, as the hour was already late, He went out to Bethany with the twelve. (Mark 11:11)

Jesus stopped and stayed overnight in Bethany many times on His way to and from Jerusalem. (He never spent the night in Jerusalem.) This is mentioned in Matthew 21:17 and 26:6; in Mark 11:11, 12, and 14:3; in Luke 24:50; and in John 11:1 and 12:11. Bethany was the home of Lazarus, Martha, and Mary (and Simon the leper, perhaps their father). I am grateful to Frank Viola for noticing and wondering about this interesting fact; he even wrote a book called *God's Favorite Place on Earth*. The word "Bethany" means house of the afflicted and house of figs, a very interesting fact as well. Simon was healed of the affliction of leprosy, and Lazarus was raised from the dead. The fig in the Scriptures is a symbol of Israel itself and the subject of key stories concerning the gospel, law, and grace as well as the return of Christ. Why was Bethany Christ's favorite place? Because He was welcomed and loved there and because He could be Himself there, which "fed" Him and enabled Him to feed those who lived there. Christ is still looking for such places today, places in the heart of believers who welcome Him in the same way that the home of those who dwelled in Bethany did. Think on these things.

Entering In

Someone must serve as tinder
For the Spirit's fire to burn;
A catalyst to enter,
To His flaming Presence turn…

Dry, sold-out souls to ignite
And create the needed heat;
Glory of worship to light,
The Son aflame in His Seat!

Your people shall be volunteers in the day of Your power; in the beauties of holiness, from the womb of the morning, You have the dew of Your youth. (Ps. 110:3)

You therefore must endure hardships as a good soldier of Jesus Christ. No one engaged in warfare entangles himself with the affairs of this life, that he may please him who enlisted him as a soldier. (2 Tim. 2:3-4)

The night is far spent, the day is at hand. Therefore let us cast off the works of darkness, and let us put on the armor of light. (Rom. 13:12)

The Lord is always looking for a David or a Jonathan (1 Sam. 14)—those who are so sold out to Him that they will step out to face the enemy no matter the odds or circumstances. And because they are willing, others will see and join them. Psalm 110:3 seems to indicate that just such men and women will volunteer and step forward to face the enemy as the time for Christ's return approaches—volunteers, willing hearts in the day of His battle. Hallelujah for such love, zeal, and bravery!

Greater than Eden

The Kingdom will Eden exceed!
A new race will emerge,
Offspring of the last Adam's seed,
With new earth will converge...

For a thousand years Satan bound,
Unable to afflict;
Glories of the Lord will astound,
Grace reign without edict!

But as it is written: "Eye has not seen, nor ear heard, nor have entered into the heart of man the things which God has prepared for those who love Him." (1 Cor. 2:9; Isa. 64:4)

Then I saw angel coming down from heaven, having the key to the bottomless pit and a great chain in his hand. He laid hold of the dragon, that serpent of old, who is the Devil and Satan, and bound him for a thousand years; and he cast him into the bottomless pit, and shut him up, and set a seal on him, so that he should deceive the nations no more till the thousand years were finished. (Rev. 20:1-3)

The old serpent, Satan, will have no direct influence on those who dwell on the earth during the millennial reign of Christ. He and all those spirits and demons who follow him will be put away for the entire thousand years. That alone will make the earth during Christ's reign far greater and more glorious than it was in the

Garden. Some resident flesh will linger in the natural hearts of the humans there at the end of the Millennium, for when Satan is released for a short time, many will be deceived and follow him! But those who have been glorified and rule and reign with Christ will follow the Lamb wherever He goes and do whatever He says. Again, hallelujah!

Kingdom Renovations

How much will the Lord renovate
When to reign He appears?
The new heaven and earth must wait
For a full thousand years…

But overcomers glorified!
Instantly made like Him,
All that's not Jesus will have died…
Pure glory transforms them!

Behold, I tell you a mystery: We shall not all sleep, but we shall all be changed—in a moment, in the twinkling of an eye, at the last trumpet. For the trumpet will sound, and the dead will be raised incorruptible, and we shall be changed. (1 Cor. 15:51-52)

Beloved, now we are children of God; and it has not yet been revealed what we shall be, but we know that when He is revealed, we shall be like Him, for we shall see Him as He is. (1 John 3:2)

Oh, what a glorious day that will be! So far as the earth is concerned, I am sure there will be extreme renovations: pollution eliminated, clean air and water, ghettoes and poverty things of the past, etc. But the main improvements will be spiritual in nature: overcomers will be given glorified bodies like the Lord's when He emerged from the tomb. They will become triumphant over sin, death, Hades, and Satan. To know Him as we are known by Him will require an extraordinary transformation! Only these will be fit to rule and reign with the Lord during the Millennium. Again, what a glorious day to look forward to! Even so, come quickly, Lord Jesus!

Afterword

Jesus is coming! Are you ready? Have you made the necessary preparations for His arrival? Scripture makes it clear that the world as we know it is a creation of Satan and fallen man, and is passing away. A new creation is on the way! If we want to be part of it, this is what we must be preparing for. As believers, we must come to see that this fallen world is not our home. The world in its current condition is a creation of Satan and fallen man, and only the coming of Jesus could change that. Christ crucified—on this and this alone is the foundation of the gospel and the Kingdom.

Long before the creation of man, all things were perfect. Heaven was God's Kingdom, and all the angels were the Father's faithful and loving subjects. But then catastrophe hit: one-third of the angels led by the archangel Lucifer rebelled. He was not satisfied being the highest of the angels, next to God Himself. He decided he must be as God, equal in power and majesty with the Most High. Ezekiel 28:14-15 describes the fall of Lucifer like this:

> You were the anointed cherub who covers; I established you; You were on the holy mountain of God; you walked back and forth in the midst of the fiery stones. You were perfect in your ways from the day you were created, till iniquity was found in you."

Isaiah 14:12-15 also speaks of Lucifer's rebellion:

> How you are fallen from heaven, O Lucifer, son the morning! How you are cut down to the ground, you who weakened the nations! For you said in your heart: "I will ascend into heaven, I will exalt my throne above the stars of God; I will also sit on the mount of the congregation on the farthest sides of the north; I will ascend above the heights of the clouds, *I will be like the Most High.*" Yet you shall be brought down to Sheol, to the lowest depths of the Pit. (emphasis mine)

Monumental pride! That was and is the sin of Lucifer, now called Satan. So the Kingdom of heaven was disrupted, and Satan and a third of the angels were cast down to the earth. Something needed to be done to re-establish God's absolute rule over all things. The Godhead's solution was the creation of man, created to defeat Satan and take back the earth.

> Then God said, "Let Us make man in Our image, according to Our likeness; and let them *have dominion* over the fish of the sea, over the birds of the air, and over the cattle, *over all the*

earth and over every creeping thing that creeps on the earth." (Gen. 2:26, emphasis mine)

Man was given dominion over all the earth, including Satan, to subdue and return it to God. That is why the very first part of the Lord's Prayer reads, "Thy kingdom come, thy will be done, on earth as it is in heaven" (Matt. 6:10, KJV). For this is the Lord's heart and desire. But of course, man fell to the same sin as Satan: to be as God. The serpent successfully seduced both Eve and Adam to rebel and become independent from God. So just as Lucifer had been cast down from heaven, man was cast out of the Garden and the presence of God, left to wander the earth as an outcast and vagabond.

The ordained plan of God (absolute rule) was delayed but not forsaken or changed. He would still use man to achieve His purpose. For centuries, He looked for a man who would fully submit to His will and commands. Many "good" men came and went, but all fell short of the man He was looking for. So in the fullness of time, the Father sent His own Son as a man to accomplish all He had ordained.

Jesus not only overcame as a man but had to die in the place of man as the perfect sacrifice for sin. To confirm that the way back to God for man has been accomplished, the Father poured out the Holy Spirit to indwell all those who come to faith in Christ. The penalty for sin was erased by the shed Blood of Jesus and the power of sin overcome by the indwelling Life of Christ. All believers are now to live by that Life, by Christ being released to do the work of God through them and by living in such a way so as to hasten the return of the Lord and the building of His Kingdom. This is the next step in achieving the eternal purpose of God. Therefore, our whole purpose here on earth as followers of Christ is to prepare for the return of our Savior and King, to be prepared ourselves, and to help others to be prepared. We are to be an integral part in re-establishing God's absolute rule over all things. And this will only come about when we, His people, make Christ all in all and the sum of all things. Amen, maranatha, and even so, come, Lord Jesus!

Other Works by the Author

Silly Snake Rhymes...and the real stuff (Children's Book)

*From the Garden to the Kingdom:
God's Eternal Purpose, Plan and Provision*

Pilgrimage: Finding the Way Back Home

Songs of a Son: Heart-Cries Along the Way

The Calling

True Identity: A Believer's Full Inheritance in Christ

Bella's Umbrellas (Children's Book)

listen|imagine|view|experience

AUDIO BOOK DOWNLOAD INCLUDED WITH THIS BOOK!

In your hands you hold a complete digital entertainment package. In addition to the paper version, you receive a free download of the audio version of this book. Simply use the code listed below when visiting our website. Once downloaded to your computer, you can listen to the book through your computer's speakers, burn it to an audio CD or save the file to your portable music device (such as Apple's popular iPod) and listen on the go!

How to get your free audio book digital download:

1. Visit www.tatepublishing.com and click on the e|LIVE logo on the home page.
2. Enter the following coupon code:
   1109-1714-19a1-b66a-e0d9-1684-29ad-fb61
3. Download the audio book from your e|LIVE digital locker and begin enjoying your new digital entertainment package today!

CPSIA information can be obtained
at www.ICGtesting.com
Printed in the USA
FFOW01n2147130916
27612FF